# RICK RO
## The Entrepreneurial Wisdom

**By Jacenna Marie Grisby**

# CHAPTER 1
# FOREVER IMPRISONED

"Twenty years to life without the possibility of parole."
I stood behind the defense table, close to my criminal defense attorney, where convictions and sentences had been handed down for decades. I looked up at the federal seal above the judge's head on the wall. I was hopeful that the judge would be impartial. I was expecting a harsh penalty, but not this one. Not in real life. When the judge hammered the gavel on his desk's hardwood block, it seemed like a hammer falling on my head, a nail in my coffin. I was sent there at the age of 36, with no way of getting out. I was going to die in prison.

It was November 1996, nearly a year after I had been imprisoned as a result of a government sting operation. A handful of the same federal agents and sheriff's deputies who had hounded me for years were in the courtroom gallery to witness the judge lay down my punishment. I knew the court couldn't legally restrike me while the sentencing hearing was still going on. Because I had not committed three different offenses for the same offense, the three-strikes legislation did not apply to me. For some reason, my lawyer did not agree. So there I stood, stoic, accepting my life sentence and powerless to change it. My eyes briefly locked with my mother's as I was carried away in chains by US marshals at my side. She sobbed, and all I could hear were her sobs. My jailers processed the conviction and registered me as inmate number 05550-045 in the federal prison system. It was official; I was going to die in jail. That helpless sense of being powerless over my own life didn't last long. I realized I had to get working and fight for my freedom, even if it meant doing so from behind bars. I was determined to find a solution. I was up to the task.

The challenge I faced was convincing the United States Ninth Circuit Court of Appeals that I had been over-charged and over-sentenced in both state and federal court. Until then, I had been imprisoned in a federal holding facility in downtown San Diego. I stared out the window of my ninth-floor cell and reflected on where I had been and where I had come from. As I settled in to complete my time, I had numerous opportunities to reflect on the route that had taken me to a federal jail. I was on the ninth floor of the Metropolitan Correctional Center, overlooking San Diego Bay. I'd risen to the top of the drug trade, regularly earning six figures, with plans already in the works to exit clean, with assets and respectable business ventures in place. Then everything came crashing down. I was now serving time in prison. I felt far apart from my past as I stood behind bars. As a young lad growing up in the beautiful hills of East Texas, I never envisioned the twists and turns my life would take. It had begun simply enough. But one experience from my upbringing stands out above the rest. And I'll never forget it.

# CHAPTER 2
# BRUTHAS AND BULLETS

I put my hands over my ears, attempting to block out my aunt's sobs. I clenched my fists, tried with all my power to block off the terrible scene in front of me. Nonetheless, I could see Uncle George's eyes riveted on the ceiling. Aunt Bobbi Jo's sobs could still be heard. In 1966, I was six years old. That's when I lost my innocence. Uncle George, my mother's brother, took on the role of a father figure for me. He drove me to a drive-in movie theater. We raced in his '63 Buick. He occasionally took me to work with him on the trash truck he drove for the city of Los Angeles; it was exhilarating, despite being noisy and always stinking of garbage. I saw the world from his garbage truck, from the downtown Los Angeles skyline to the Watts Towers. Uncle George grew on me. He rose to become my hero.

My mom and I lived with Uncle George and Aunt Bobbie Jo for the first three years of my life, until she earned enough money to support us. There were also difficult times since Uncle George was a heavy drinker with a short fuse. On his way home from work, my Uncle George would stop at a nearby bar. He got home drunk one evening and accused Bobbi Jo of meeting other men. Uncle George became furious the more Bobbi Jo denied it.

He yelled, "Don't lie to me, bitch!" "You think I'm a toy, don't you?" That's exactly what it is. "You think I'm messing with your ass?" Then he snatched a steak knife from the kitchen counter and stabbed Aunt Bobbi Jo. The point of the blade sliced through her top and into her left breast like butter. Bobbi Jo screamed and struggled to free herself from his grasp. He merely pushed her down tighter, nearly breaking her in half with the sheer power of his weight. The knife struck her again, this time severing her shoulder. My mother yelled at him to let her go, but he refused. Mama was carrying a small-

4

caliber pistol at the time. I believe it was a.38. I don't recall her pulling the pistol and pointing it at my uncle, but he must have seen it in her hand because he came to a halt and backed away.

"George, I don't know what the fuck your problem is, but you got to leave here! Now!" Mama hollered at him.

"Why you gettin' in our business, woman? This here ain't got nothing' to do with you!"

"Fuck that! You have lost your mind if you think I am going to stand here and let you kill that girl. Just go, George."

"Okay. I'll leave," he shouted as he turned and looked at my aunt, "but it's not over, Bobbi Jo. I'll be back." Then he stormed through the living room and out the front door.

Mama visited Bobbi Jo. She sat at the table, trying to balance her shoulder and chest. The front of her clothing was stained with blood. There was blood on the floor and in the sink. I stopped just outside the threshold, tears streaming down my cheeks. I'd never seen that much blood before.

"Girl, we've got to get you to the hospital," Mama said to Bobbi Jo.

"Annie Mae, why did he have to do this to me?" Bobbi Jo murmured, her voice shaking. "Doesn't that man realize I love him too much to play with him?" What am I going to do, sweetie? "What should I do?" She began to cry.

"You're going to get your stupid ass out of here, that's what you're going to do." Then Mama said to me, "Come on! "Ricky, let's go!" Mama grabbed Bobbi Jo's arm and helped her to her feet. I followed them out the rear door.

I stayed as near to Mama as I could in the dark and cold. We crossed the backyard into an alley, which led to a three-story apartment complex from the 1950s. We dashed through the gate, up the backstairs, and out of the shadows. During our brief escape, Bobbie Jo left a trail of blood. Her breathing was strange, as if she had a cold.

"C'mon, baby." Mama encouraged her. "We are almost there."
We walked up the stairs to the apartment of Mama's friend, Jimmy D. Mama pounded on the door. From inside, an apprehensive voice asked, "Who there?"
"It's me, Annie Mae. Open the door, Jimmy D."
"That you?"
"Yeah, dammit, it's me. Open the door!"

We all poured into Jimmy D's modest one-room flat when a frightened Jimmy D swung the door open. It smelled like stale cigarettes and stale beer. Jimmy D, a modestly built man with a huge afro, saw the blood on Bobbi Jo's blouse and almost passed out from the shaking.

An anxious We all poured into Jimmy D's modest one-room flat once he swung the door open. It smelled like stale cigarettes and stale beer. Jimmy D, a modestly built man with a huge afro, saw the blood on Bobbi Jo's blouse and almost passed out from the shaking.
"Thank you, Almighty God!" Bobbi Jo, what happened to you?"
"What happened to her was her jealous husband." "Come on, help me stop the bleeding," Mama said.
"What did he do to her?"
"He slashed her. Jimmy, could you please get some clothes or something to stop the bleeding?"
"Yes, yes. "Wait here," he murmured as he walked into the bedroom.
I sat on the couch, watching what was going on. Looking back, I see how simple it is for children to accept the actions of adults as usual. We as children regard them as normal, no matter how exciting or horrifying they are, because what the adults around us do is all we know when we are little. Mama and Jimmy D spent 10 minutes finding and bandaging Bobbi Jo's chest and shoulder wounds. Uncle George stabbed her three times, leaving open wounds that required stitches. We hadn't been there 15 minutes when Uncle George arrived.

Bam! Bam! Bam!

"Open the door, Jimmy," George hollered as he pounded on the door. "I know they in there!"

"Oh, God! Oh, God! Please, Jesus!" Bobbi Jo moaned.

"C'mon. Quick. Over here," Mama whispered to Bobbi Jo and me.

As Mama grabbed my hand forcefully and led me out through the living-room window onto a little patio, Jimmy D assisted Bobbi Jo. Jimmy D drew a yellowing window shade down and closed the even dirtier curtains across the shade, blocking our view. Uncle George could be heard ranting through the front door. Jimmy must have leaned on the door while opening it, since the door smashed into the wall as if someone had slammed into it. Out on the terrace, Mama and I were as quiet as church mice. Bobbi Jo was so still that I believed she'd ceased breathing. We heard George shut the front door and pound his feet across the apartment floor, opening and closing the living room closet door. Jimmy D was cursed and threatened. Jimmy D pleaded with him to calm down. "George, you know I would've told you if they were here. C'mon. Don't break anything, man."

"Shut up!" George screamed. "I'm leaving, but if I find out you had them up here, Jimmy D, I'll put a stump and mud hole in your ass." We didn't move as we heard the front door slam behind him as Uncle George left. Bobbi Jo began to groan. A lone beer can rolled on the concrete lane beneath us. The drapes sprang open, and the window shade rose. Jimmy D seems to have seen a ghost.

"Y'all gotta leave here, Bobbi Jo," he said. "I don't know what he thinks you've done, but he's mad as hell. You can't stay here."

"Bobbi Jo hasn't done nothin', Jimmy. George needs to quit drinking is what he needs," Mama explained. "Furthermore, he needs his black ass kicked!"

"Well, nobody doin' no ass-kicking 'round here. Y'all got to go!" Jimmy D said.

"You know we don't have a car, Jimmy. Could you go down to the phone booth and call a cab?"

"Yeah, but go on out to the downstairs and wait for the cab."

Jimmy D led us out of the apartment and down to the first floor apartment lobby, where he dialed the cab company. The street outside the glass doors was calm. We waited over 30 minutes for the taxi to arrive. I was no longer afraid at that moment. I was exhausted and chilly rather than afraid. Mama was still furious, and Bobbi Jo was still afraid. When we got to Charles Harper's, Mama's boyfriend's house, Charles nearly fell through the roof. Charles entered the kitchen and pushed the front of Bobbi Jo's shirt up. We could all see the fat layer beneath her skin via the gaping incision. The gravity of the situation became clear to me at that point. Someone had hit me in the chest. I started crying again.

"Don't worry, baby, everything is going to be alright," Mama said, putting her arm around me. I turned and looked up into her strong face and tried to smile, but tears streamed down my face. That was when Uncle George kicked in the door. I just about jumped out of my skin. Uncle George stormed into the apartment like a raging bull. Charles stood in the kitchen doorway trying to block Uncle George from walking in. But he was noticeably smaller than George; he probably weighed 20 or 30 pounds less.

"George, there's no fighting in my house," Charles said sternly.

"Outta my way, nigga," George responded. "Bobbi Jo! Get yo' ass over here. Now!"

Bobbi Jo got up from the chair. I couldn't believe it when she started to go to him. I cried even harder. Mama stepped between Bobbi Jo and George.

"No, girl, stay out of this," Bobbi Jo told Mama.

"You stay outta my business, bitch!" Uncle George hollered at Mama. "Get over here, Bobbi Jo! Don't make me tell you again!"

The next few moments are a kind of fog. All I remember is after Uncle George slammed Charles into the wall next to the kitchen door, Mama pushed Bobbi Jo and me back, away from them.

"Please, Jesus. Please, Jesus. Pleeease, Jesus!" Bobbi Jo sobbed.

Then I heard a thunderous sound.

BOOM!

Uncle George stopped in his tracks, looked down at his chest, and fell like dead weight into the kitchen doorway. Mama had shot her brother George dead. Then she went to jail. Nothing would ever be the same again after that day. Nothing.

The cops arrived, followed by an ambulance. When the cops tied Mama and took her out the door, putting her in the backseat of a patrol car, I burst out laughing. I had no idea if I'd ever see her again. Charles then led me to his mother's house, which was in front of his converted-garage apartment. The thundering sound of gunfire echoed over and over in my head as I wept myself to sleep that night, like a broken record. Bobbi Jo was discharged from the hospital the next day, but I stayed with Charles' mother, who looked after me. I hadn't seen Mama in a long time, although it was probably only a week or two before she was released, after investigators found she'd killed Uncle George in self-defense with a single gunshot wound to his chest. We moved out of Bobbi Jo's and into an eight-unit apartment building on West Cordova Street not long after Mama was discharged. It wasn't a home, but it was ideal for just the two of us.

We moved to a little, white three-bedroom house in South Central Los Angeles a few years later, bordered by freeways from the 110 to the 405, and the 10 to the 105. My mother and Auntie Bobbi Jo had a shared desire of purchasing a home. Near the corner of 87th Place and Flower Street, the house was quite close to 110, also known as the Harbor Freeway. The 110 was the inspiration for my friends to rename me Freeway Rick years later. The 110 cuts through the geographical divide in Los Angeles between the haves and have-nots. Later, to widen the 110, they used eminent domain to take my mother's property at 430 West 87th Place. It was the same year I was incarcerated.

Uncle George had a severe dispute with my mother the year before he died, hitting her and permanently knocking out one of her eyes. She's got a glass eye. After the attack, George hid in Texas for a year before returning to California, where he stayed until the day of the shooting. Uncle George had bought Mama a rifle a few years before to keep her safe while she was living as a single mother with her children in the harsh L.A. 'hood of South Central. She fatally wounded her brother with the same rifle he'd bought for her. Mom and I had adjusted into our new existence on 87th Place.

# CHAPTER 3
# JOURNEY TO THE CITY OF ANGELS

I am a slave's descendent. My mother often told me about her great-grandfather, Mike Britton, who worked as a slave for a Texas farmer, and her great-grandmother who picked crops beside him in the fields. He became a sharecropper once slavery was abolished. They were a strong, hardworking family. Mike Britton's son, who was also my great-grandfather, retired from the railroad. My first three years of life were spent in Arp, Texas, a small, mostly wooded community near Tyler in Smith County with a population of roughly 800 people. My elder brother David and I were living on the outskirts of town with our mother, Annie Mae Ross. I had no idea where my father was. And at the time, it didn't matter to me. But I'd find out where he was soon enough. My mother had bought a modest two-bedroom cracker box for $1,600. The windows in the front faced the highway. It contained a modest living area, a small but functional kitchen, and only one bathroom. The house wasn't much to look at—we were poor—but it was home, and that was all that mattered. My brother David and I were content.

Opal, an older white woman known to local children, owned and ran the small petrol station and store on her own. Opal treated everyone with respect, usually smiling and saying something nice when they came into her store. I recall pedaling my tricycle back and forth to Opal's store, hauling a large red wagon, with my dog Pooch jumping around by my side. I drank the sodas and ate the free cookies she appeared to have in abundance. I'm not sure how she made a living with her somewhat decrepit shop, but she was always giving away free food. Doris, my mother's dearest friend, lived a bit further down the road. Mom and I would walk to Doris's little shack of a house on weekdays when David was at school and when the weather was nice. We sometimes remained all day. Doris had a son, Keith, who was also one of the only kids my age nearby for miles to play with. Keith was my best friend, except for my brother. We didn't have much, but what we did have was pleasant and always clean, and it felt more than enough to my three-year-old mind. Given her limited resources, Mom made our lives as pleasant as she could.

Few people came to our house because of the considerable distance between houses in the portion of town we lived in, which was more country than city. We only saw individuals inside the automobiles rushing by on the highway. My mother had a lover, but neither David nor I were particularly fond of him. We avoided him whenever he came over. When Dad wasn't there, it was just Mom, David, and me. Our father had abandoned us not long after I had turned three. Living in a rural region of town offered our small family lots of time to spend together. My mother and I were inseparable when she wasn't at work or when David wasn't in school. When my mother wasn't there, David and I had a great time playing indoors and outside. David and I weren't just brothers; we were great friends. I not only admired him, but I also adored him. Because we lived so far out in the country, David and I were frequently left alone when Mom went into town for work. We did practically everything together, and David was always available when I needed him.

David and I would be separated before the end of 1963 and would not see one other again for eight long years. It was a traumatic occurrence in our young lives. The breakup occurred after school one day. I was too young to legally attend school at 3-1/2 years old, but the school had permitted me to accompany David a few times, most likely because my mother didn't want me home alone while she worked because I had been involved in what fortunately turned out to be a minor traffic accident. I had a minor head injury that required stitches, and I was still wearing the bandage. I recall that the school desk chair was too high for me to sit on, so I had to climb into it. When some of the girls in the class babied me during lessons,

David's teacher would get irritated. The girls coddled me because I was always little for my age, which upset the teacher. When school concluded that day, David's teacher exhaled a breath of relief and dismissed class for the day. I had no idea it would be the last time. We skipped, jumped, and laughed all the way home. My mother halted David and me in the living room with a stern verbal command seconds after we came through our front door, still laughing and talking loudly. "Go to your room and start packing your clothes and toys." Take Pooch. "We're relocating to California."

Except when David went to school, our dog Pooch followed us everywhere we went. I had no idea where or what California was, yet moving wasn't the most surprising thing. It was the news that followed, that David would be staying in Texas with our father, who, for the first time, resided not distant from us. I burst out laughing when our mother announced that David wouldn't be joining us.

Texas was deemed a racist state in the 1960s because blacks still had to say "yes, sir" and "no, sir" to white people. California provided more prospects for blacks in the South, and Mom wanted to give us the best chance for a prosperous life. Her only option in Arp was to clean houses, which was a restricted possibility. She desired more for herself and her children. And if that meant separating David and me for the time being, then so be it. We took David and his belongings, as well as our dog Pooch, to our father's place. It was the first time I'd seen my father in years. I had forgotten about him until that point. Before I knew it, my mother and I were at the Greyhound Bus Station in Arp, preparing to catch a bus that would take us to our new home in Compton, California, in southern Los Angeles, sometimes known as South Central L.A.

We arrived at Aunt Luretha and Uncle Johnny Wilson's residence in the afternoon. Ted, Bennett, Evita, Rene, and Yvette were their five children, who were of different ages. My cousins were still in class when we arrived. I met them for the first time when they returned home. That was a huge advantage of relocating to California; I discovered cousins I had no idea existed. They became my pals. Mom would occasionally take me with her when she was looking for a job. I believe that's when she realized that leaving Texas didn't guarantee she'd be free of racism; despite the California sunlight, palm trees, and positive image, our skin was still dark. I spent a lot of time alone while my cousins were at school after she got a full-time job and her work hours extended. For me, being alone was a novel experience. But it wasn't all unpleasant during our brief stay with Aunt Luretha and Uncle Johnny.

Mom and I quickly packed up our little items once more. We moved out of Aunt Luretha's home and into the home of my mother's brother, Uncle George Mauldin, and his wife, Aunt Bobbi Jo. Mom and I each had our own bedroom, which was preferable to a living room with a couch. Uncle George and Aunt Bobbi Jo had two younger children, George Junior (aka Tootie) and Kenny, who became more like brothers than cousins. Life became a never-ending episode of fun, games, and enjoyment for me from the minute we moved in with Uncle George and Aunt Bobbi Jo, which I had previously experienced in Arp, Texas, with David. It was as if I'd known my cousins my entire life. The pain of losing David was quickly overcome by joy at having little relatives to play with.

Life at Aunt Bobbi Jo and Uncle George's had been lovely up until that moment. I was having so much fun as the days and months grew into years that I almost forgot about Arp, Texas, and my life with David. I didn't realize it at the time, but the good days at the Mauldins' house were about to come to an end. The manner I lost Uncle George has been with me for the rest of my life.

# CHAPTER 4
# GROWING UP IN 'HOOD'

It was a classic California day—warm with a gentle wind. And nothing unusual happened at St. Lawrence of Brindisi Parish Catholic School, where we went about our everyday business. That is, until the midday break. There was no way those of us in the schoolyard that afternoon could have imagined that an event that was about to take place would have such a significant impact on my life. It all happened during a game of marbles.

Watts' St. Lawrence Catholic School first opened its doors in 1924. It was only two streets from where the Watts race riots occurred in August 1965, causing six days of chaos. While other structures were destroyed, St. Lawrence remained standing. My mother was able to enroll me there rather than in public school. She wanted me to have an excellent education and believed that the nuns who worked at the school would do the greatest job. Shooting marbles was the most popular sport among the St. Lawrence guys, including myself. It was the most fascinating game I'd ever seen. I gathered hundreds of marbles of various shapes, sizes, and colors. There were the dark, mysterious pearlies and the lighter, multicolored cat's eyes. There were the massive, rocky boulders and the tiny, mostly solid-colored peewees. Every day, we fired marbles all day. We played at morning, noon, and before we departed for home at the end of the day. All of the youngsters understood that when we played, it was for real—or so we thought. It was dubbed "keepsies."

Even though we could buy a bag of mixed-color marbles for a quarter, finding the highly sought pearlie or aggie in a store-bought bag was rare. They had to be won, but they weren't always readily won, even if they were won fairly and squarely; battles may erupt. This day would be no exception. Our location was big and covered in fine sand. Dennis drew the pot after we smoothed away the top layer of sand. It was quite large, maybe three feet broad. I smiled when I noticed that enormous pot. We could tell by the size of the circle that the pearlies, aggies, and bumblebees were going into the pot. The wider the circle, the more difficult it was to knock out the marbles—unless you were good. And I was fine. Steelies, the little ball-bearing marbles found inside spray paint cans, were not used because they could damage the glass marbles. Boulders were also not permitted.

With one shot, a single boulder might knock out three to four marbles from the pot. They were feared by everyone. Nobody knew where Dennis acquired his marbles, but he always had the best and most beautiful. I couldn't wait to see what he'd placed in the pot that day. Dennis was two years older, bigger than the rest of us, and had a habit of flaunting himself whenever there was a crowd around. He dug inside the front pocket of his short pants when he was sure he had everyone's attention—everyone at St. Lawrence Catholic School wore the standard Navy-blue shorts, white shirt, and checkered vest sweater.

I preferred to go last and usually stayed back to better observe those I had to defeat. Dennis looked at me as though he was saying, "You better not win the lag or I'm going to beat your little ass." He was well aware that if I won the lag and shot first, his chances of getting a decent shot were limited, and his bumblebee would be mine. I bent my waist slightly and swung my arm backward just enough to give my stone the push-roll. It was a lovely cat's eye with swirls of gray, brown, and yellow. It was the perfect size for my little fingers. I threw it away. My cat's eye, on the other hand, rolled up the slight ridge in the soil where Bird made the line. It teetered for a split second, causing me to stand up with my fist balled. Then it slid down to the line and came to a halt.

I was first, and Dennis' bumblebee was just as good as mine, and everyone knew it, including Dennis. I smiled at Dennis and moved forward to retrieve my cat's eye. But Dennis had a different plan. He just stood there, astonished, staring at the pot for a time. Then he bowed down, grabbed up all the marbles in one hand, and dashed through the crowd, shoving some of the kids to the side and knocking some of the girls down.

My last day at St. Lawrence was that day. I'd already been in a few fights, and for reasons unknown to me, I'd developed a serious spelling and writing problem about the same time. Both difficulties, school authorities informed my mother, rendered me unsuitable for St. Lawrence. My mother's hurtful expression when she arrived to pick me up from school that day has stayed with me. I could hear and see my mother's sadness in her words and in the way she stared down at me as we left St. Lawrence for the last time, shortly after I was expelled. My mother's ambition of sending me to Catholic school had been dashed. I was immediately perplexed when I learned that I would not be returning to St. Lawrence. When I overheard my mother tell Aunt Bobbi Jo over the phone that she'd have to locate another school for me, I had no idea what she meant. I had no idea what the distinctions between public and Catholic schools were. When everything was eventually explained, I wanted to jump for delight. Deep down, I felt giddy with joy. There will be no more uniforms. There will be no longer three daily prayers. There will be no more strict rules.

I grew up in a pious Baptist home and was baptized in that faith. The sisters refused to let me join in communion with other children because I was not Catholic. I felt left out, sitting alone on a bench outside the chapel, wondering what I'd done wrong and hoping it would all be over soon. I was relieved that I no longer had to put up with that. My expulsion meant something entirely different to my mother. I didn't know why at the time, but I could see it in my mother's eyes, her sad demeanor, and the slowness in her speech. It was painful for her to see me expelled after she had worked so hard to get me into Catholic school in the first place. It was significant to her on numerous levels.

My mother and I were part of the black migration that began in the 1940s after World War II from rural Southern states to the West Coast in search of jobs and a better life, only to be denied access to the suburbs and confined to blighted communities in East or South Central Los Angeles, which included Watts and Compton. Except for Aunt Bobbi Jo, who adored me like her own son, and my younger sister, Angie Richardson, my mother was all I had. She was born when I was seven years old and was also scheduled to attend St. Lawrence. That was now on the line. I could feel my mother's pain, which had all started because of my fight with Dennis James. Looking back, I know it was at St. Lawrence Catholic School that I first got depressed. I was punished for doing what I thought was right by standing up for my classmates and myself. I also felt like an idiot for not being able to meet the desired educational requirements.

My mother enrolled me at Manchester Elementary School, which is located on Manchester Avenue between Hoover and Figueroa avenues. My cousins went to the same school as me. In comparison to St. Lawrence, Manchester was a wild new world. I relished my newfound freedom, free of the stringent regulations of Catholic education. The sole obligatory ritual at Manchester Elementary was reciting the Pledge of Allegiance; there was no getting down on our knees to pray. School had now become a place where I eagerly anticipated attending every day. Even though I struggled with an ever-worsening writing and spelling difficulty and my new teachers battled over how to remedy what they assumed was a learning handicap, I thought public school was fantastic. My mother appeared to be satisfied with me while she established a life for us in California. My remaining two years in elementary school were uneventful in terms of my peers. I got through fifth and sixth grades without getting into a big fight.

It was a completely different story for teachers. In class, I behaved out. The inability to read and write were significant hindrances. My mother had previously attempted to teach me to read and learn my ABCs when I was four and five years old. Reading was the furthest thing from my thoughts, and I had no idea how damaging it would be for the rest of my life. I'd already begun to rely on my physical ability rather than my thinking abilities. Around that time, my mother began referring to me as a leader. My mother even hired two tutors for me. One of them was a lovely girl named Taylor. I enjoyed visiting her house. She did get some work out of me; I was a sucker for the gorgeous ladies even back then. But I struggled with spelling, reading, and writing. Even now, it's difficult for me to write, but I force myself to.

I learnt a few tactics in school by acting out to avoid having to read. It got so terrible that the school suggested I seek psychiatric assistance, such as seeing a doctor. I once went to see a large man in an office on Century and 74th Street. He was a county evaluator, and he questioned me about why I was acting up at school. While still a student at Manchester Elementary, an incident occurred on the way to school one morning with my cousins Kenny and Tootie, as well as two friends, Maurice and Terry, that once again disrupted my life to the point where I felt saddened, frightened, and insecure, just as it had after my mother was arrested for the murder of Uncle George. All of the bewilderment, dread, and uncertainty I felt that night washed over me like a tidal wave.

The school year had come to a conclusion, and the summer of 1972 had begun. With the zeal of wild birds finally released from captivity, we looked forward to the sun and freedom from school. My brother David also moved to California from our father's house in Texas that summer to live with Mom and me. I was relieved to see not only my big brother, but also my best friend. I had someone to chat to and play with at home for the first time in a long time. Summer was a time for the beach, and with the California coastline only a half-hour away by car and not much longer by bicycle, I was glad to have David back to join in the fun. We went to Playa del Rey, Santa Monica, and Venice beaches.

That summer of 1971 was also the beginning of my discovery of my athletic potential. With my rising confidence and strong desire to succeed, I dedicated myself to learning how to play football with the same zeal and zeal that I had dedicated to being a master at shooting marbles. That summer was full of fun. David played varsity football for Fremont High in the Watts area that fall after school started. We played catch in the street when David wasn't practicing football or going to school. I became proficient at intercepting the ball. When neighboring guys my age played with us, it didn't take long for me to stand out. A vacant site at the end of the block was ideal for a football field. At the end of the games, beaten, bruised, and tired, we'd return home, complaining about the mistakes someone else made if our block lost, and the cursing and name-calling would begin all over again. If we won, the swearing was followed by laughter and trash talk about who had the best touchdown or catch. Football was the focus, and it was a lot of fun. Two of the players in those games, Allie, nicknamed "Killer," and Derek "Dee" Brown, became friends with me. They resided on 89th Street between Broadway and Grand, yet they played football with our block's squad. Then there was Terry Bowman, the first person I met after we moved to 87th Place. We first met in the alley behind his house while I was on my way to Burger Dan's, a little hamburger shop run by Miss Betsy down the street.

After spring practice at Fremont High concluded, my brother began scrimmaging with the varsity football team in preparation for the impending football season and the start of the new academic year.

Meanwhile, in June 1971, I was promoted from Manchester Elementary, along with others my age from the neighborhood, and we began making our own plans for the approaching move to junior high school. Most of us would be attending Bret Harte Junior High. I was afraid, not just nervous. Sure, there was always a sense of exhilaration and nervousness associated with starting a new school. Moving up from elementary to junior high, although signaling maturation and growth, also meant entering a school with an infamous reputation, and I dreaded the day I walked onto the campus of Bret Harte.

If there was one period in my childhood that had to be remembered as the genuine start of my adolescence, it was September of 1971. Although I'd never become a legitimate member of the infamous Crips street gang (as in signing a pledge of membership), through association, I'd become as much a member as any of the most devout originals. I became someone other than an ordinary homie spewing ghetto slang; I became someone entirely different from the person I'd formerly been. I never ran the streets with gangbangers, but I grew up in the same neighborhood as them. I was 13 years old at the time, and I believed it was my destiny to become a Crip.

# CHAPTER 5
# GANGSTERS, GUNS, AND HOMIES

My first day at Bret Harte Junior High, located at 92nd and South Hoover streets in the heart of Watts, I was convinced I was going to see firsthand why Bret Harte was one of the most feared junior highs in the Los Angeles Unified School District. I was pleasantly delighted, though, by a dull, unremarkable day—that is, until the final bell rang at 3:30. I spent the majority of the day, along with hundreds of other new freshmen and returning students, filling out documents related to registration and class selection, as well as getting acquainted with the school premises. Because I'd learned them, I could write my name and address on the forms. That was the limit of my writing ability at the time. First period was homeroom. Although I didn't know any of the kids in the homeroom at first, I quickly became friends with Frank Jones, one of the founders of the 107th Street Crips and one of the most dreaded kids at Bret Harte. Frank, also known as Moomoo in the gang, was as big as a bull and as tough; he was notorious for bench-pressing 290 pounds. Moomoo was the coolest person in my opinion. I also made friends with Darrel Rainier, who was also a member of the 107th Street Crips, as well as Anthony Edgar and Jeff Hill, two of the few lads in the homeroom who weren't gangbangers but were tough enough to hold their own. Anthony would go on to become one of the most talented football players at Bret Harte (now known as Bret Harte Preparatory Middle School). Mr. Vick, my homeroom teacher, was cool and liked by everyone. He spoke in our language, with our slang and phrases. That first day, after homeroom, I went to the following three courses and tried to memorize the directions to each one.

I didn't eat much that day because I was still worried about being at school. I stood around looking at girls and trying to remember which kids I knew. After lunch, the day was filled with additional classes, talking, sitting, signing documents, and receiving assigned textbooks. The bell rang, signifying the conclusion of sixth period and the end of the school day. As students filed out into the hallway to their lockers, I assumed that my first day of junior high would be like any other average day, and that all the things I'd heard were much exaggerated. I even informed one of my local homeboys about it. I spoke too quickly. I walked out of the building, putting my books in my locker, approaching the north gate, looked up, and nearly peed my pants. At least a hundred lads were congregated inside and outside the north-gate entry, as well as on the sidewalk that surrounded the back of the schoolyard, with no teachers in sight. The throng closed off the street right beyond the gate. They'd have to get out of the way for me to pass. That would never occur to me.

I was terrified. They'd chase me if I turned around to walk the other way. I continued going blindly, almost in a fog. Even yet, I knew instinctively that if I showed fear, I'd never be able to hold my head up in class again, and it was only the first day. I observed someone I recognized as I got closer to the gathering, my heart beating. Leon Washington came from the neighborhood and went to Manchester Elementary with me. He was known in the gang as "Baby Bam." But I knew him as Leon in school. He was also watching me while conversing with one of the gangbangers. I tried to appear casual as I moved forward slowly. After our brief conversation, I exhaled a sigh of relief. Out of the corner of my eye, I observed that the guys standing about the yard, staring, were trying to figure out how I knew Baby Bam.

When Leon walked away from the crowd with me and we headed home, I felt even more confident. Walking along 92nd Street made me feel brave. Later, I felt safe if I watched someone's money or leather coat being snatched by gangbangers, which was usual when a non-gangster got caught on Crip land. I performed no better academically in seventh grade at Bret Harte Junior High than I had throughout grade school, as I continued to struggle with spelling. I couldn't understand simple ABCs no matter how hard I tried or how much time a teacher spent helping me. I hated science, English, and history subjects and only tried hard in plastics shops and physical education. However, I did fairly well in arithmetic. I've never struggled with numbers. It was a skill that will come in good later in my career.

When it came time for me to move on to eighth grade, junior high followed in the footsteps of elementary school and easily passed me. I assume some of my teachers felt sorry for me and thought they were doing me a favor by moving me along. I was 12 years old at the time, and it didn't matter—at least not to me. I was content as long as there was a gym to play basketball in, a field to play football and baseball on, and my buddies to hang out with. I didn't realize how difficult I was making things for myself as I approached maturity as an illiterate.

In January 1972, I grew more connected with the Crips, almost joining them. Outside of individuals who resided in my neighborhood, the majority of my buddies were already gangbangers. I gradually wandered away from home and onto the streets. Without realizing it, I was becoming as tough and callous as many of the gangbangers I used to despise. But an incident in eighth grade forced me to change my mind and reconsider what might happen as a result of my increasing contact with 92nd Street Crips members. Many gangbangers at Bret Harte came from various sets of the Crips. The gang members I was involved with belonged to the 92nd Street clique.

The early 1970s — 1970, 1971, and 1972 — marked the start of one of the most volatile eras in South Central Los Angeles history in terms of gang evolution, an increase in violent gang-on-gang action, and a reign of terror and bloodshed over the impacted communities.

A number of other black youth gangs evolved from South Central's vastly underdeveloped, stagnant, and furious ghettos, and many became as notorious as the LA-based Crips. None, however, achieved the global fame, large number of members, or longevity of the Crips.

By mid-1973, the 92nd and 107th Street Crip gangs had almost fully taken over my school. Though a small number of Denver Lane Bloods remained, the majority of Denver Lane gangbangers had either been forced out or graduated. Bret Harte was a dangerous school for those who weren't Crips; for those who were Bloods, it might be lethal. I'll never forget the one occurrence that forced me to take a long, hard look at myself. It was the first time in my young life that I began to question my soul about the path my life was undoubtedly on. My friends Jeff, Moomoo, and I strolled down the main corridor to our lockers after classes one day. I stopped at my locker first and dialed the combination to my lock.

I stowed my stuff, locked my locker, and spun around to find myself gazing down the barrel of a.38-caliber pistol. I froze in fear. I was unable to move or speak. Sleepy, a member of the Denver Lanes gang, held the gun inches from my brow, and I glanced at his angry eyes, as if he was about to shoot me. Because he was wearing a deep-red kerchief, or bandana, that covered his mouth and lower face, all I could see were his eyes. Moomoo and Jeff were not to be found. When they noticed Sleepy and another gangbanger approaching us, they immediately fled. We waited there for what seemed like an age, no one moving, no one saying anything. I stared breathlessly ahead as Sleepy held the gun to my head. Everything became alarmingly evident at that point, even down to the rounds within the gun's cylinder.

Finally, Sleepy and his buddy simply turned and went away, which was surprising. It was over as quickly as it had begun.

I carefully searched the streets I had to walk down, first in front of me and then behind me, the entire way home. My thoughts never stopped racing. I walked as fast as I could without bursting out in a sprint. It was strange, because even though I knew I was terrified, I seemed to have gone into a kind of stupor for those few moments, where everything around me vanished and all I could see or think about was the barrel of the pistol, the copper-colored shells, and Sleepy's leering face. All sound came to a halt.

I made a conscious effort to remain calm once I was in the protection of my own home. But then, as if on cue, thunderclaps. It began with the image of a lifeless, bloated body floating in Manchester Park's swimming pool. Then I saw Uncle George's face, his mouth and eyes wide open, staring towards the ceiling. It made me never want to carry a gun or even own one. At that point, I resolved never to join a group again. Indeed, I avoided most contact with gang members. I couldn't stop thinking about how close I'd come to being shot in the head—for no reason other than being in the wrong place at the wrong time, in the school hallway. I'd seen how dangerous gangs can be, and I didn't want anything to do with them.

# CHAPTER 6
# ARTHUR ASHE'S SUCCESSOR

I began playing tennis around the time I became disillusioned with gangs. The time was ideal. Prior to tennis, my main interests revolved on sports that I was too tiny to excel at, such as football, basketball, and baseball. Aside from being threatened with a pistol, an instructor we called Doc was responsible for my decision to stop racing around South Central as a full-fledged gangster, which would have resulted in an early death or a hefty prison sentence. I might not have played if I hadn't been open to trying something new. I met Coach Richard Williams one weekend after a group of 20 people gathered at Manchester Park to convert one of the park's four tennis courts into a roller rink. We tried to pull down the court's net by grab-assing in and out of it like the Los Angeles Thunderbird roller-skating team.

Doc arrived with racquets and a large basket of tennis balls at that point. Although we'd seen Coach Williams around Manchester, no one in the group had met him previously. He was, in fact, the one who brought tennis to the park. We initially horsed around by throwing balls at each other. Doc then offered a dollar to anyone who could hit the ball over the net into a box he'd set up. We pushed ahead like a pack of wild beasts, or just the young guys we were—the same homies who'd later become known as the "Freeway Boys"—yelling and declaring first position. Doc explained the game's objective, and we attempted to hit the ball. We'd changed the racquets into hockey sticks and the balls into pucks by the end of the day as we played our own version of tennis. Tennis, as far as I could tell, was not a sport played by tough young black lads. It wasn't as physical as football. I saw it as a game played by girls and wealthy white folks.

Doc, who worked for the parks and recreation department and coached tennis at Manchester, was introduced to us by Coach Williams. However, my dear friends Larry, Tony, Robert, and Terry not only began training with Doc, but they also began receiving gifts of shoes, tennis suits, racquets, and wristbands. In no time, Robert was ranked 14th in the state and Larry was ranked 20th in their age categories. I considered the state of California. I was impressed, so I joined up to play as well under Doc's supervision. I worked hard at tennis, which I no longer thought was only for girls, and gradually progressed.

Robert, a 10th grader at the magnet school Dorsey High, suggested I speak with his tennis coach, Larry Smith. If Robert, a statewide ranked player, thought I was a good enough player, then maybe, just maybe, I'd finally found a sport where size didn't matter. I took Robert's advice and approached Coach Smith after school one day. I promptly tracked down Mr. Smith. We talked about the game, and then he encouraged me to practice with the high school squad after school. I was overjoyed! I was barely out of junior high when I was offered a chance to train with a real tennis team, just a few months after discovering a sport in which I could succeed. I couldn't believe my good fortune. To make matters even better, another friend, in addition to Robert, was already in the squad. The fact that Robert had discussed my abilities with Mr. Smith before my appointment with Coach had to help. Nonetheless, the meeting with Coach Smith went well.

I began practicing with Dorsey High's tennis team whenever I could while still in junior high. By the end of the 1974 school year, I believed I had a strong chance of becoming another great black tennis player, possibly as successful as Arthur Ashe. I tried to persuade myself that I didn't need a college education or outstanding grades to accomplish that aim. Even though I couldn't read, I was promoted from Bret Harte Junior High School in June 1974. I now had a junior-high diploma, despite having done very little to get it. I had three years of junior high and six years of primary education, yet I was still illiterate. But all that mattered to me was that I played above-average tennis.

Other than a few scrapes after I first attended, Bret Harte Junior High had not lived up to its reputation as one of the toughest schools in Los Angeles. It was no more frightening to me than elementary school. I'd obtained a pass from the 92nd Hoover Street Crips while at Bret Harte Junior High, which meant they left me alone. Despite the fact that the gang problem persisted throughout Los Angeles, including in my area, my fear of them became nothing more than a passing notion. It was difficult to totally avoid Los Angeles' expanding gang problem, which infested every neighborhood. I had few gang-related friendships and had little problem avoiding risky areas. It had become something I heard about in the news or from friends, rather than something I had experienced. What mattered to me was that I wasn't a part of it. I was 14 years old, holding a diploma, and I felt I was on my way to a wonderful high school, a tennis career, and a bright future.

# CHAPTER 7
# TICKETS FOR MEALS

In September 1974, Robert, Larry, Tony, Terry, and I boarded a city bus bound for Dorsey High School, all at the request of Coach Larry Smith and using the addresses of friends and relatives who resided in the district. After the first day of classes, the four of us dashed to our lockers, stashed our books and notebooks, and dashed to the gym to change into our tennis attire. It was our school year's first formal team practice. Doc, who continued to work with me at Manchester Park when I wasn't practicing with Dorsey's squad, made sure I had new tennis attire and high-quality equipment, which he paid for. I had been working out with the squad for months before school started, and I was already in tenth place.

To make the varsity team, I'd have to be in the ninth or lower slot, and the competition was fierce. To get the job, I needed to advance to varsity, which I knew wouldn't be easy. My new friends and teammates, including Moss Cart, Louis Lane, Tony Wingo, Reggie Stanton, and Reggie Bass, were all fantastic players. That first session was intense as we competed for a spot on the team. It was thrilling. We spoke about who beat who, who was the better player, and each other's flaws and strengths on the bus journey home. Each of us, according to our own lofty expectations, was well on his way to becoming the league's top-ranked player, despite having yet to play a single league game. We were filled with the youth's innocence and confidence. I didn't have time for school, homework, parties, or even females. Tennis consumed all of my free time and consumed all of my energies. It became my way of life.

I played well enough in 10th grade at Dorsey to make junior varsity, a level slightly below varsity but above B-level players. I quickly established myself as a dominant force on the JV squad and was soon permitted to compete in singles matches with the varsity team. With that, I established a trustworthy reputation among some of the team's key players. And Coach Richard Williams was interested in me and spent time offering me advice. They eventually placed me in special education at Dorsey, and everyone in the class was embarrassed to be seen walking to and from the Special Ed building. We rushed in and out of the classroom, hoping no one noticed. My tennis coach assisted me by prodding me along, not realizing that he was actually slowing me down. Despite my illiteracy, I completed a driver's education course and obtained my license. Robert obtained his license as well, and when his parents purchased him a car, our school bus rides came to an end. I started saving the money I would have spent on bus tickets. I had extra money for the first time in my life. I soon discovered a profitable way to invest my savings: meal tickets.

Your family had to be poor to qualify for meal tickets, which were county-funded vouchers that supported hot lunches cooked by the school cafeteria. It was considered a dishonor at Bret Harte to use the "welfare tickets"—as they were known back then—and embarrassing if you were one of the unfortunates who had to do so out of necessity. The majority of Dorsey students came from middle- or upper-middle-class families and did not qualify for the meal-ticket subsidies. So it seemed strange to me that students who were financially well-off really needed meal tickets, in part because the meals were better—with more variety and greater portions—than ordinary cafeteria fare, and it was hip to trick the system. Whatever the reason, the tickets were in high demand, and I had them. All I had to do was buy tickets from disadvantaged Bret Harte students. They were more than delighted to collect money for something they were embarrassed to use, and I made a profit by selling the tickets to those who could afford them. For the first time in my life, I was making money from my own business. I'd never felt such financial independence and delight as I did with those few extra nickels, dimes, and cents. I still had money left over after buying all the sodas, pastries, and sweets I could consume. It was a pleasant sensation.

Our varsity team was seeded third in the city of Los Angeles at the end of 10th grade, and we were on our way to the playoffs. We overcame Van Nuys High, a top-four school, in the first round. Terry, our top varsity player, defeated Vance Van Patton, Van Nuys High's greatest player, in a hard-fought game. Then came Birmingham High, and Terry once again saved Dorsey by defeating Birmingham's greatest player, David Robinson, in another tight game. Although the varsity squad had performed admirably in the previous two rounds, they were heavily trounced in the third round of play by Palisades High, effectively ending the season. Junior varsity had not performed as well and did not make the playoffs, but we shared in the varsity squad's accomplishment. I didn't know how to handle losing because I'd never played organized sports before, other than in neighborhood vacant lots. I was devastated, but I was even more motivated to return the next year and earn a spot on the varsity squad to help the team win the championship.

Jim Kelly, a rising martial-arts film star with a dojo (a tiny martial arts studio) on Crenshaw Boulevard, was a frequent visitor to the famed park. Tennis star Arthur Ashe worked out there as well. Bill Cosby, a TV and movie star at the time, was known to frequent Rancho's tennis courts. Larry and I met Kelly, the young black Kempo Karate expert, at Rancho. Jim frequently went to the park to jog or play tennis. He observed Larry and me playing tennis one day. He introduced himself, expressed his admiration for our ability, and invited us to whack a few balls with him. I knew then that tennis was the sport for me. It was the correct thing to do if someone like Jim Kelly played. Kelly began commenting on how much better players Larry and I were compared to other partners he'd practiced with, and how much he enjoyed playing with us after a few practice sessions, much to our delight. We quickly became buddies. I recall Jim's excitement when he received his first Porsche 911. It was rapid and it was black on black.

He gave Larry and me a ride home from the park one day, so we crowded into the small car. I'd never been in a Porsche before, and it was exhilarating to see how fast he drove. I was out of breath from excitement, but also a little worried the whole trip home; I just knew the cops were going to pull us over for speeding. Larry and I were deemed cool after that day. Overall, during my first year of high school, I was a member of a team that came close to winning the city title and met a real-life movie star and karate expert who drove a Porsche. Life was fantastic, and it was all because of the game of tennis.

The varsity team made the playoffs again during my junior year. Although we did not win the tournament the next year, we did deliver a crushing loss to Hollywood High, whose team was mostly white and considered one of the greatest at the time. Our team, which was not expected to do well against them, won 7-0, deflating the tournament and media buzz surrounding the Los Angeles School District's prima-donna team. During the playoffs that year, I met Norman Tillman, one of the few black players for Hollywood High at the time. Everyone expected Hollywood High to easily defeat not only Dorsey but any other team. When we destroyed Hollywood with Norm on our side, we found it incredibly amusing that Norman seemed to share our triumph excitement with just as much verbal fervor as the rest of our team. Norman and I had become friends by the conclusion of the school year. Not only did he live in South Central, but his brother was a Hoover Crip and a member of one of the Crip gang's most recently organized divisions.

I finally made the singles varsity squad my senior year at Dorsey. Things were going well until the playoffs, when we were brutally defeated by Birmingham High, a white high school in a rich L.A.

Valley community just off the ocean. I couldn't believe we'd just lost to a team we'd beaten earlier in the season. To make matters worse, it occurred during the first round of play, before my match. I was heartbroken. I didn't want to go to school any longer. I was nearing the conclusion of my senior year and vowed not to continue. But, even though I wanted to, I didn't stop going, and I didn't tell my mother about it. The ultimate decision came soon after I spoke with a Long Beach State University tennis coach, who had invited me to his campus to discuss after seeing me play a match earlier in the season against a guy ranked third in the city. The chat was going well until I told him the secret I'd kept from so many others.

I'll never forget how the coach stared at me oddly. It seemed as if I had suddenly developed a terrible odor. Coach was silent for a few moments before saying, "There is no way you can attend Long Beach State." My illiteracy appeared the most repulsive thing he'd ever heard, based on his words and his furrowed brow and squinted eyes. I felt awful, like a loser. Tennis had promised me a bright future, but with Coach's few words, it was gone, and with it, my ambition of becoming a professional tennis player. To make matters worse, my illiteracy quickly spread, and everyone at Dorsey High knew what I'd told Coach. Even kids who didn't go to Dorsey had heard about it. The ultimate blow came when Richard Williams, unintentionally, embarrassed me to the point of tears when he handed me a newspaper on the tennis court and pointed out an article he wanted me to read. Of course, I couldn't do it, and it was in front of a lot of students, so I felt humiliated. School ended for me at that point. I dropped out of high school near the conclusion of my senior year, not long before graduation.

# CHAPTER 8
# PARTY SUMMER

It was the summer of 1978, I was 18 years old, and I had dropped out of high school. I didn't immediately inform my mother. When I finally told her the truth, she was not pleased. To her, I was a slacker with no education, no career, and no hopes for the future. I couldn't figure out where I'd gone wrong. I'd been hitting balls with Lawrence "Cornbread" King, a tennis great ranked second in the United States for National Parks. He was a fellow dropout who, like me, had struggled in school yet went on to become a successful player; all of this strengthened my idea that I could achieve the same. I was sure I had some talent if someone as talented as Lawrence King had asked me to volleyballs with him. It turned out to be the reverse, and I became depressed. I quickly returned to hanging out with my homies Ollie Newell, Wayne, Bruce Dog, and Tootie, who spent the most of their time smoking pot, drinking beer, and low-riding.

Then the summer got out of hand. My mother declared her intention to visit Texas and asked if my cousins or I wanted to accompany her. She estimated that we'd be gone for around two months. Nobody wanted to leave. We didn't want to leave Los Angeles. We knew it would be exciting to have the entire house to ourselves. She wasn't bothered by it. She packed her belongings, stocked the refrigerator, gave my cousins and me money, and went to Texas. It was party time as soon as she stepped out the door! We had the entire house to ourselves, unlimited food in the fridge, and nothing but free time on our hands. All that was missing were girls and beer.

On the corner of 87th and Broadway, Thrifty, a hybrid appliance, drug, and food shop, sold everything from bread and Pepto-Bismol to TVs and fishing paraphernalia. When one of us needed something for free, we would gather 10 to 15 guys and storm the store. One guy slunk away from the group and wandered from aisle to aisle, seeming to be watching the camera, as if he was scoping out the scene. While the manager kept an eye on him, the rest of us hurried out the door with cases of beer, bottles of wine, and bags of potato chips. We were generally laughing so hard that it was difficult to run. We got so proficient at it that we relocated to the Safeway on Manchester and Hoover and tested our new method there. We partied and raided the markets for two months like we had a license to do whatever we pleased. People would sometimes crash in the garage or outside behind the house after all-night parties because they were fatigued from dancing, drunk from drinking beer and wine, and zoned out from using marijuana. The party resumed the following day at that location. Someone may occasionally stray home. Otherwise, they would have stayed the entire summer. Even though I'd dropped out of school and had no plans for the future, it didn't matter to the homies. I used to be somebody. My homeboys would have gone to great lengths for me, and I would have done the same for them. The summer of 1978 ended when my mother returned from Texas. Mom was tough on me. Everyone else, including my homeboy Ollie and cousins Tootie and Kevin, was getting ready to return to school. Not me. I had nothing planned until I learned about a community college that provided adult-education vocational classes.

Mr. Dan Foster, an auto-upholstery instructor I met while playing tennis at Rancho Park, suggested that I learn a skill after learning that I had dropped out of high school. He recommended going to the institution where he taught auto upholstery. I decided to go after some thought, especially since Mr. Foster stated I could be paid to go. I felt vehicle upholstery could be a useful talent to acquire because low-riding was becoming more fashionable, and with it, personalized auto interiors. I asked for and received a grant from the Education Equal Opportunity Group, and I enrolled in Los Angeles Trade Technical College in September 1979.

Trade Tech was a medium-sized junior college located immediately south of Washington Boulevard on the fringes of downtown Los Angeles, between Figueroa and Flower avenues. It was a well-known, long-established two-year college with a diverse student body from many ethnic origins. It provided a variety of trade and university preparation classes. Norman Tillman had also registered at Trade Tech, and I later discovered that Lawrence "Cornbread" King had attended as well. Most importantly, Trade Tech had a strong tennis team. Norman and I eventually started playing together again, and we both made the squad. Rather than taking up auto upholstery, I decided to attend bookbinding classes for no apparent reason. I soon found myself working on a trade I had no idea existed. Junior year and high school were far less fascinating than Trade Tech. Aside from practicing tennis and competing against a much more accomplished and better all-around set of players, I was blown away by the freedom of movement that a college campus provided.

My mother didn't care what classes I took; she was simply glad I was back in school. I was, in fact, in school, this time at the collegiate level. And I couldn't even read or write. I met a girl called Marco a few months into the academic year. It was the first time I'd had a genuine interest in the opposite sex, owing to my self-consciousness about my appearance. Despite my best efforts to tell myself that it didn't matter, I had a hunch my height did. Or perhaps I was even ugly, I reasoned. Marco was on the girls' tennis team, and I hung around in a semi-private place, close enough to view every aspect of her but far enough away to avoid detection. She had short hair, cocoa-brown skin, an athletic body, and a pleasant demeanor. But I soon got a little further with her. We began practicing together and had a good time. Because she also lived in South Central, she would occasionally give me a lift home after school. My gaze was fixed on Marco.

I was the only one without a girlfriend among my friends and family. My brother had one, as did my cousins. I wanted to be able to boast that I had a stable girl. That would make me look cool, I reasoned at the time. One of my buddies informed me, much to my dismay, that the girl of my dreams was a lesbian. That was the end of my first, albeit one-sided, love affair, as well as the academic year. Trade Tech's second year was a carbon copy of the first. When tennis season ended, I stopped attending school and returned to hanging out in the hood with my homeboys, doing nothing. My college experience ended just as quickly as it began.

With the summer of 1980 in full swing, I discovered a new passion: hanging out at carhops. Carhops were gatherings of low-riders who partied all night in a park, a hamburger shop, or a large parking lot. Low-riders from Los Angeles, Compton, Pasadena, and the San Fernando Valley arrived in a variety of vehicles, primarily Chevys, Fords, Buicks, and pickups. Some had lifts, some didn't, but they were all dressed out with women: tall women, small women, gorgeous women, and not-so-pretty women. Carhops were in, and they quickly became my thing. Girls didn't appear interested in me until I met carhops, and I was too nervous to approach them. If my male juices had remained dormant up to that point, my luck was about to change with so many gorgeous, sexy, barely clothed girls congregating in one area. Young women were now irresistible and easily accessible. I had completely forgotten about tennis and school. All I wanted was my own girl. It didn't matter what she looked like unless she wore short skirts and a wonderful scent. I didn't give a damn. I only needed a relationship.

# CHAPTER 9
## '66 CHEVY CONVERTIBLE

To say I was unskilled with women would be an understatement. The truth was that I had no prior experience. After hanging out at carhops and Church's Chicken, I realized I needed a car to get a girl—at least the type who kicked it with low-riders at the carhops. That was the deal. I saw some of the most beautiful women with the most hideous niggas at carhops. When I saw a lovely female with a tight-rounded butt, creamy skin, and thick thighs hanging out with a dirty, large, hulk-looking guy, I couldn't believe it. It wasn't hard to figure out why: it was his automobile. The cars at carhops were alluring. When the lovely paint was exposed to light, it shone like diamonds. While sitting in the sumptuous custom-fit mohair, velvet, and velour interiors, the low-riders' favorite songs were pumped out over costly sound systems. That didn't stop me from purchasing a vehicle. I soon found a destroyed '66 Chevy convertible at a Long Beach junkyard. The car had no engine or transmission and a large dent in the quarter panel on one side.

I bought the junker and coaxed the yard into towing it to my house with the $100 I made supporting pimps on Figueroa by watching the backs of their whores while they turned tricks at seedy motels. My mother couldn't believe I paid $100 for a worthless pile of metal. I knew nothing about cars when I started breathing fresh life into the shell of my '66 convertible. My friend Ollie, who worked at Downtown LA Motors, assisted me. Furthermore, the same young blacks who grew up in the 'hood and were gangbangers and vehicle thieves were suddenly auto mechanics, electricians, and auto-body workers; some even ran chop shops full of stolen automobile parts. My shell of a car had a great operating engine, a half dashboard, a red front, and one black and one blue door in no time. It appeared to be a car that had been stolen, stripped, and abandoned on the street to rust, but it was gradually springing to life. When I got my '66 to the point where it could be driven, it was time to get it juiced. A thrilling aspect of low-riding was getting a car juiced, raised, and hopped. When the option to have my own automobile lifted presented itself, I jumped at it. However, hydraulics, or lifts as they were usually known, was a completely separate science than auto repair. Attaching hydraulic fluid-filled cylinders to the A-arms of an automobile's front axle, cutting out and reinforcing the rear frame, and installing pressure pumps required an expert, and I wasn't even close.

Athen Nelson, the man for the job, was not only the finest authority on hydraulic-lift installation, but also the man to see if you needed a quick laugh. Despite his oddities, Athen Nelson was a nice guy— short, slender, black as night, 120 pounds soaking wet, and hilarious. Everyone I knew who was into low-riding hung out at his house. Athen and I spent a lot of time together in 1981, the year I was introduced to low-riding and ladies. While Ollie and I were at Athen's, an incident occurred that brought me back to my days at Bret Harte Junior High and my worst gang experiences.

Ollie and I were kicking it with him at Athen's while he worked. Ollie has been making decent money at Downtown LA Motors for some time. He'd spent $400 on a new set of gleaming rims. Ollie's and my automobiles were both parked at Athen's. Donnie Young, a member of the Imperial Court, or PJ Crips, and a handful of other buddies from the 'hood, as well as Jake Clayton, a member of the 62nd Street crew, a new gang established from older and former Crips members, were also at Athen's that day.

Jake gave me the nickname "Freeway Rick," a play on the name "Junkyard Freeway Boys" that he'd given to Ollie, Wayne, me, and the other boys who lived in my neighborhood near the Harbor Freeway. He was an automobile and parts thief who was looking to steal Ollie's car. Everyone was standing about on the driveway the other day, talking stuff and listening to Athen crack on one of the men. Jake was pointing a gun at Ollie the next thing we knew. Ollie and the rest of us in the driveway were stunned, staring at Jake as if he were insane and about to shoot us all. Jake treated us as though we were utter strangers, and he was holding us up. Everyone went very still. I was hesitant to move since I wasn't sure if Jake was serious.

Donnie was all over Jake before he could grab him. Except for me, everyone else in the driveway ducked for cover as Jake and Donnie fought over the rifle. I stood immobilized, helpless to do anything but hope the pistol didn't accidentally murder me. The guys rushed Donnie and Jake, breaking them apart, with the gun no longer in Jake's possession and no one in risk of being shot. Jake went without saying anything when everyone had cooled down. It reminded me of the day when Sleepy from the Denver Lanes pulled a gun on me at Bret Harte Junior High School. Even though I wasn't directly involved—I was simply at the wrong place at the wrong time—it terrified me because it happened so rapidly, before I had a chance to flee. I couldn't even tell you how it all started. Sleepy had smiled as if he, too, was just playing that day, returning the revolver to his waistband and walking away as if nothing had happened. Another narrow escape.

Not long after, we were kicking it in the driveway of Athen's business when Donnie spotted Jake Clayton cruising by. Donnie, still enraged by Jake having a gun to Ollie's head, pulled out his weapon and started fire on Jake's automobile. Donnie was lucky not to strike Jake or an innocent bystander, because the police arrested me for it. They claimed I was the head of the Freeway Boys, so the officers linked my name to the shooting and arrested me for assault with a deadly weapon, despite the fact that I had nothing to do with it. I was in jail for 72 hours until they released me without prosecuting me, and then they arrested me again for the same act a few days later, claiming fresh proof. The district attorney eventually reduced the charge from a felony to a misdemeanor. At the preliminary hearing, Jake Clayton, who was designated as the victim, did not appear, and everyone knew I wasn't the shooter, so the D.A. dismissed the case and I beat the charge.

My mother was still hovering over me, constantly pressing me to get involved in constructive activities. I hadn't told her about my time at Athen's garage because of the sometimes-illegal nature of his business. She assumed that when I quit attending Trade Tech, I hadn't gained any skills that would lead to a job. She was correct. While I wanted to make money, I lacked the abilities to go out and get a good career. With nowhere to go, no one special to go with, and no money for gas, I ended myself working as a carhop at Church's Chicken on Vermont and Century at least three times a week. The majority of the time, Ollie, Wayne, Bill, and I traveled together. We parked around the corner, but our cars were still an embarrassment in comparison to the carhops' elaborately painted, expensively modified, and sophisticatedly equipped show cars. "White Boy Eric," a light-skinned black with the cleanest '64 Chevy Impala, was one of the carhops. Eric, the White Boy, became my hero. He was a "jumper," a guy who competed with low-riders from different parts of town at carhops in interior design, paint jobs, and hopping contests.

The Burger King on Crenshaw and Jefferson was a regular stop for the carhops after they left Church's. It was a block outside the authority of the Los Angeles County Sheriff's Department but within the jurisdiction of the Los Angeles Police Department. Despite the fact that the majority of young blacks I knew thought the LAPD was prejudiced against blacks—particularly low-riders—the LAPD was better than the Sheriff's Department, which had a well-publicized history of beating and sometimes killing blacks inside its patrol area.

That's how it went. Ollie and I spent more and more time at the carhops. My '66 had a long way to go before it was considered a low-rider. A girlfriend seemed equally out of grasp. But that would soon change.

I started going to church with my mum around this time. I'm not sure why. Perhaps it arose from internal conflict. Or I felt bad about turning to a life of crime. Perhaps it was the stress of being charged with auto theft and not knowing whether I would go to jail or not, even though the case was eventually dismissed due to a lack of evidence. I wanted to do the right thing for whatever reason. I was determined to give it a shot, so I went to church. But it was also at that little improvised chapel that I met Sharon. It was difficult to talk to her alone at church because there were usually people around, but I chased her nonetheless. Sharon quickly became my obsession. Sharon was a resident of 47th Street. I hopped on my 10-speed bicycle and arrived at her front door in about 15 minutes. We spent hours each evening, from around four until nine, just before Sharon's mother got home, hugging, kissing, and groping. I was confident that my luck had finally changed. Sharon, the beautiful young lady of my fantasies, was my girlfriend.

Because of my friend Dirty Benny, I started making money by working at a chop shop. The term hardly scraped the surface of his disheveled appearance. Dirty Benny's raggedy attire was always soiled and smelling, and his dark skin appeared to be covered with a layer of grease and dust. Dirty Benny, on the other hand, was more than a greaser stereotype. He was the best vehicle thief in town, as well as the finest at chopping cars in his shop with an acetylene torch. My dreams of being the Arthur Ashe of my time and playing professional tennis were permanently destroyed in return for the chance to make $50 and become a car thief.

That same night, at around 2 a.m., I found myself in a Westside Los Angeles area playing lookout as Dirty Benny used a snatch bar to break into the Seville so TQ could use the front end for components. I was driving down the street in a stolen Seville within minutes. I'll admit, I was nervous. As I drove down the street, it seemed like all eyes were on me. I kept looking around, expecting to see cops charging at me with sirens blaring, lights flashing, and guns drawn, just like on TV. It did not occur. After a few blocks, I calmed myself and focussed on getting to Benny's chop shop on Hooper. I was quickly turning into Benny's driveway. The garage door slammed shut behind me, cutting off the street noise and barring anyone from entering. I was overjoyed. My first experience with auto theft went off without a hitch. It had only taken 10 minutes to find the automobile, start it, and drive away. It was the simplest and quickest $50 I'd ever made. Benny, ready for the job in his typical soiled grease-monkey costume, put on his welder's hood, lit up his torch, and began chopping off the front end of the Caddy as soon as I got out of the car.

I was enthralled by the procedure and fascinated by Benny's surgeon-like ability as I watched him shred the once-elegantly made machine. It was a significant offense to pull that off. And I knew what I'd done was wrong. However, having money in my pocket made it easier for me to ignore that crucial aspect. Later that morning, I informed my friends about the theft and showed them the $50 I'd received. Ollie "Big Loc" Newell and my cousin Tootie, whom I referred to as my brother, both agreed it was fine. That made me feel better, and I quickly forgot about my earlier concerns and feelings of guilt. I was now a legitimate auto thief, and there was no turning back. Dirty Benny, his buddy Jumping Jake, and I were back at it the next night. Dirty Benny had been paid $300 per stolen automobile by a Bakersfield man, and Benny asked if I wanted to help for $100 per car.

For two months, Benny, Jumping Jake, and I stole nearly every luxury, sedan, compact, and sports automobile ever produced. We drove the cars to Benny's, where they were either split out or delivered whole, depending on the buyer's preferences. It was a straightforward yet effective system. I made decent money and learned more about automobile disassembling than I ever could have in school.

Soon after, Dirty Benny was arrested for theft (GTA, or grand theft auto), and his earlier parole was revoked. He was returned to prison. I simply moved in and took over, not knowing whether he had relatives and with no word from Benny himself on what to do with his shop. I enlisted the help of a few of my homeboys and began teaching them exactly what I had been taught only months before. It wasn't long before I was joined by a new group of eager young auto thieves and cut-up dudes. We grew in the absence of Dirty Benny, and under my leadership, we abandoned Dirty Benny's location and created my own chop shop.

The shop thrived, and I was once again making a good living. My '66 Chevy was in good shape. I still didn't have a girlfriend, but that was fine because I kept myself occupied. Everything went swimmingly for six months until one night, while two crew members were stripping a '79 Pontiac Grand Prix, the heart-stopping sound of a police aircraft circling overhead drew our attention. Our moves were spontaneous, automatic, and instantaneous. I ran to the front of the store and peeked through the window, terrified of what I was about to witness but too afraid not to look. I became immobile. The police were swarming the area. I saw them seize Donnie, my cousin Evita's boyfriend, who'd parked his car up to the business only a few minutes before the cops pounced.

We needed to be quick because the cops were already within the yard in front of the shop. The hoodlums threw down their tools and dashed for the back door. I was confident they'd flee quickly. I dashed out of the business yard and into the neighborhood through a side entrance.

There were cops everywhere. I turned around, feeling like a confined mouse with no way out. I ran and ran and ran, oblivious to where I was going. The police aircraft hovered right over me, following my every move as relentless police officers pursued me on foot. Finally, after what seemed like an eternity but was most likely only a few minutes, I was too fatigued to take another step. I collapsed face down on someone's damp lawn and remained motionless, waiting for authorities to apprehend me. When one of the officers caught up to me, he elevated his foot and planted it on the back of my neck. More officers arrived. I was handcuffed and thrown into the rear seat of a black-and-white police cruiser.

That is exactly what occurred. I was chained on a bench inside the station and grilled within an hour. Despite my best efforts, the queries all had something to do with what was going on at my shop. After approximately a half-hour, the police shackled me to the bench, where I sat for what felt like hours. There was no clock visible to me. I was exhausted and uneasy, and I had lost count of time. When the officer returned, he and another uniformed cop were accompanied by my homeboys Donnie and Ollie, as well as "San Jose Mike" McLoren, my chop shop co-partner. I was taken aback to see Ollie.
"I know you guys were stripping cars in that garage," the cop stated to the four of us. You're all going to be prosecuted with grand theft auto since it's a chop shop." We didn't say anything. While he was asking us questions, another cop came in and whispered something to him. The officer interviewing him then turned to the uniformed officer accompanying him and stated, "Book 'em."

We were softly led through a hefty metal door into a small, gate-topped holding tank. We were removed from the holding tank individually, me first, and walked to the booking area. We were photographed, fingerprinted, and sent to a secure cell. We were given a pay phone to make collect calls once we completed our booking documentation. I contacted a bail bondsman whom we all knew. Mike and I were back on the street a few hours later after making bail. Not long after that, Ollie was gone.

Donnie, on the other hand, believing that the police had no case against him or us, elected to remain in detention until the preliminary hearing rather than waste money on bond, assuming that his case would be dismissed before it ever reached court. I believed, for no apparent reason, that my chances would be greater back on the street. I was desperate to seize even the smallest advantage. With prospective prison sentences looming, we all agreed that going anywhere near the business would be a bad idea, given it was most definitely being observed. We didn't want to add to the evidence the cops already had on us. True to his forecast, the criminal case against Donnie was promptly dismissed, as was Ollie's. However, Mike and I were charged with felony grand theft auto and running an illegal vehicle chop shop.

Our public defender had us all plead "not guilty." Then came the wait for our preliminary hearing, which would determine whether the case against us would go to trial. The lawyer provided us with no indication of the amount of the prosecutor's evidence against us. He thought we could win the case on the basis of improper search and seizure, but we understood that if the court thought the evidence was strong enough to bind the matter over to Superior Court, we were in big trouble.

It was exactly as the attorney had hoped based on the motion he'd filed with the court, because the police had returned to my store the night of our arrests to search it, but they didn't have a search warrant to do so properly, therefore the case was dismissed. It was over in an instant. Santa Clara As we walked out of the courthouse, Mike and I exhaled deep sighs of relief. At the same time, the arrests meant that my days of running a chop shop were over. But that was fine. It was too close for comfort for me to continue. We permanently closed the chop shop. I was liberated, but absolutely bankrupt. I went downtown and applied for general assistance, which paid $75 a month. I lacked an education, my dreams of being a professional tennis player were faded, and my future was uncertain. I was determined to do what I soon realized was "the right thing." Around this time, I was formally exposed to a different manner of producing money. Big bucks. And it was about to alter the course of my life.

# CHAPTER 10
# WHITE POWDER AND STRENGTH

Mike McLoren, a former partner in the management of my chop shop, was back in town from college. He called and invited me to his home at Adams and 22nd Avenue. Mike lived in a nice one-story home with a rear house when he was in town. Marvin Gaye lived around the corner. Mike returned home during what I mistook for a break at San Jose State to visit his parents. When we first got together, we got into a conversation about making money, which led to the game of selling narcotics. Mike, often known as "San Jose Mike," told me about how he painted automobiles to help pay for college. His earnings, however, were insufficient to meet his education expenditures. As a result, he began selling powder cocaine to his university peers. I'd only heard of individuals snorting cocaine and had no idea what the ostensibly "drug of the wealthy" looked like. From what I'd heard as a kid and from watching movies like Super Fly, I assumed cocaine was largely used by movie stars, singers, and black pimps. I'd also heard that it was used as an aphrodisiac by some ladies.

My fate was sealed that day, after that one discussion. I had no idea I'd be involved in a federal controversy concerning that white powder. Then Ollie showed up. He approached the couch where we were seated at Mike's house. Mike had a mirror, which he set on the coffee table. He sprayed the mirror with a small amount of the fine, rock-like, yellowish powder. The golden substance appeared to be solid, hard, and lacking in crumbs, with two or three huge, irregular rock-like balls surrounding it. We didn't say anything. Mike was equipped with a single-edged razor and a plain white paper straw. Ollie and I watched as Mike skilfully chopped up one of the boulders into a fine, yellowish powder with the razor. The garage was filled with the weird, heavy, and medicinal odor of the material. Mike cut the dust into even tiny bits as he continued to diminish it.

I was curious what he planned to do with it once he was finished. Mike smashed another small rock, then used the razor to cut the pile into six equal-sized flattened hills. He then expanded them into six powder lines. Mike leaned forward over the powder lines on the mirror and, with one end of a straw in each nostril, inhaled one of the lines into his nose so quickly that it was almost comical. We, however, did not laugh. Then he snorted another line and sat back, squeezing his nostrils with his thumb and index finger to keep the powder from escaping. He sniffed all the time, like he was trying to keep his nose from running, just like in the movies. Mike looked at Ollie and motioned with his hand for him to try a line. Even though he appeared nervous, Ollie imitated Mike by snorting not one, but two lines of the powder. Ollie snorted it with a grimace but said nothing.

It was then my time. Ollie and the majority of my homeboys smoked cigarettes, smoked marijuana, and drank beer. Despite their best efforts, I never felt compelled to participate. But on this particular day, my curiosity got the best of me, and I didn't want to stand out as the odd man out. So I broke my long-held record of remaining clean that day. I jumped in with the zeal of any chump who thought he'd finally found his big break. I felt nothing, much to my dismay. I felt I knew what it was all about after hearing about the so-called rich man's drug of choice and watching movies with Hollywood criminals shooting it out and killing each other over the pricey powder. Ollie and I were pushed from that point forward to learn whatever we could in order to get into the flow of money that Mike outlined. I stuffed the leftover cocaine into my pants pocket and rushed into Ollie's raggedy '64 Chevy with its damaged driver's-side door, driving west on Manchester Avenue to my ex-tennis instructor Dan Foster's house. Mr. Foster, a middle-aged man, seemed well-informed about a variety of issues, so I felt he could be interested in learning about the cocaine game. We arrived at Mr. Foster's house in the upscale West Los Angeles community of Baldwin Hills and found him removing a seat from a small boat in his backyard. Ollie and I assisted him. We got into a long conversation about the genuine purpose of our visit as we worked. Mr. Foster told us, much to my surprise, that he used to sell cocaine for a living. Being young at the time, I assumed that a man in his fifties wouldn't know the first thing about street narcotics. However, this was Mr. Foster. He revealed that he'd made so much money distributing narcotics that he'd used his earnings to tour the world in style. He sat down and went into great detail about the ins and outs, as well as the pros and downsides, of the cocaine trade.

He mentioned the dangers as well as the large fortunes to be had. He cautioned us that if we were found selling the drugs, we would go to prison, and that drug traffickers may be killed during robberies. He also mentioned the women, the houses, the cars, and the hundreds of thousands, if not millions, of dollars that could be produced. My curiosity about the small mound of powder Mike had introduced us to become an all-day quest. Ollie and I were curious to see whether our homies were interested in selling cocaine with us. Ollie locked the door behind us as soon as we walked through it. I extracted the packet of cocaine from my jeans pocket. We stopped at Irene's Liquor Store on our way west on 87th toward Figueroa Avenue to get something to eat. I saw an old friend, Barney, just inside the door, a shermhead known throughout the area who was so high on PCP that he trembled. I had no issue presenting Barney the powder inside the booze store. That shop functioned as an open market for marijuana and PCP sales. I took the baggie from my pocket and handed it to Barney. He opened the bag, dipped his finger inside it, and placed it on his tongue. "That's cocaine," Barney replied after a few seconds, pointing to the bag. "It's for real." "I knew it!" I yelled.

The following day, I swiftly contacted acquaintances and sold lines from my first gram of cocaine. I was a drug dealer in no time. I was playing a game. I was intrigued by the drug and Mr. Foster's fascinating stories about ladies, fancy automobiles, and money. But I needed more cocaine now. Ollie and I would have to spend $300 to get cocaine from Mike to sell on the street. We were about to do something stupid to acquire it, but we didn't concentrate on how stupid it was. We discovered a Buick parked behind a closed gate at Bret Harte Junior High in the middle of the night. The automobile was most likely the property of a night janitor. We wanted the wheels, not the automobile. They were eight-wires with whitewalls and Vogue yellow tires. They were all over the pimps' automobiles. Before we started working, we double-checked the area to make sure it was clear. When we were sure no one was looking, we sprang out of our car, leaped across the street, and dashed to the parking-lot gate like two desperate junkies looking for a fix. We climbed the gate, drove around town looking for a tow truck to rob. They were in plenty in Los Angeles. We'd been looking for one for almost an hour when we came across one parked in a yard on Vernon Avenue. We grabbed it. I returned to the Buick, connected it up, and towed it to the location where we planned to remove the wheels and leave the car. We located a location on a side street for the tow truck and left it there after we got the wheels.

I thought Buick would make me rich since it would bring us one step closer to getting more cocaine to sell for cash. We weren't concerned about being discovered. Police only fingerprinted vehicles if they apprehended thieves in the act of auto theft or if the vehicle was utilized in a severe crime, such as homicide. We never wore gloves because we knew the cops wouldn't lift our fingerprints. All four wheels were promptly sold for $300. We could have received $500, but all we needed was $300 from San Jose Mike to buy more coke. I was addicted to the thought of what cocaine could do for me.

# CHAPTER 11
# SHOOTOUT ON 81st STREET

The word spread quickly around the 'hood, and I made some useful connections throughout the game. It was normal business networking, with the exception that the product was not of the Chamber of Commerce sort. Pip, my cousin Evita Wilson's boyfriend, was one of the new relationships I'd met through networking.

Pip, like me, was a drug dealer, as did his younger brother, Keith. Both were Hoover Street Crips who supplied PCP, the street term for phencyclidine (chemical name phenylcyclohexylpiperidine), a powerful animal tranquilizer. It was yet another 1980s narcotic that spread throughout the black ghettos and eventually became epidemic. Pip and Keith were PCP specialists.

Ollie Newell and I decided to live with Evita. This was a wise and planned action. It enabled us to connect with Pip and Keith and learn about the drug industry from them. Furthermore, Evita lived near the 81st Street drug sales area. Norman Tillman joined my crew at that time, fresh out of the Marine Corps after three years of service. He injured his ankle while playing intramural basketball and was unable to continue. He didn't see any work opportunities other than selling some marijuana on the street. Street vendors approached a slow-moving car, clutching whatever they were selling in their hands. They were swift, slick, and quick-witted, ready to spit out a well-rehearsed sales speech at 90 miles per hour. Customers ranged from well-dressed to raggedy, sporting everything from head rags to fine jewels. Some were really youthful, while others were noticeably older. It made no difference who they were or where they were from. They were acquiring clients.

The year we lived with Evita was significant not just because it marked the beginning of my drug-dealing profession and the chaotic atmosphere on the 81st, but also because it was when my sales truly took off, as I quickly became acquainted with the key players in the area. It was a carefree era. Ollie and I spent our days lounging around listening to the radio, partying nonstop, and eating hamburgers and fries while earning ridiculous sums of money. Ollie and I learned a lot about PCP by hanging out with Pip and Keith on the 81st and watching them at work. By the time Ollie and I moved in with Evita, the sale of PCP by a significant number of black youngsters, both male and female, known as Hoover Crips, had already exploded. Indeed, the popularity and availability of PCP may have started with the Hoover Crips' turf on 81st through 83rd between Hoover and Vermont. By 1983, PCP had become a major problem in the neighborhood. Tony Stacey, Evita's prior partner and the father of her two girls, was a member of the Hoover Street Crips, a gang that lived on gangbanging adolescents trafficking the crippling PCP. Even after Tony was sentenced to life in prison, his dominance in the Crips was not diminished by his absence from the streets.

Customers new and old who wanted to get a stick for PCP's deadening high merely had to walk or drive down 81st. Almost everyone on that stretch of 81st, from Hoover to Vermont, was either using or dealing PCP at the time. Pip and Keith were key figures in the propagation of angel dust on the street, delivering a seemingly endless line of men and women, young and old, for $15 for a half-stick and $30 for a whole. The narcotic was kept in a small, transparent glass jar, which could be purchased at one of the many liquor stores that dot the neighborhood. To make a half or complete stick, cigarettes were used. When a sale was accomplished, the dealer would usually dip a Sherman cigarette, half or whole, depending on the customer's preference, into the strong, unique, chemically scented liquid.

The Hoover Crips were also based on 81st. To be honest, I was a little nervous. Despite the fact that I attended school with many of those homeboys, I had no idea what to expect from them. People are changed and empowered by group mentality. pals in our area frequently battled with pals they grew up with. Shooting and even killing each other was not uncommon if a feud erupted. I'd spent a few years away from the streets, playing tennis and competing. I had to work on being calm once I was back in the flow. I was not scared to get into a fight with someone if necessary. It was all a matter of perception when it came to winning and losing. However, in South Central, if you got into a fight with the wrong person, you had a higher chance of winning the lottery.

Still, the 'hood was the ideal location to establish my drug business, though doing so required the appropriate attitude. Because gangsters can take advantage of the weak, I had to play my cards carefully. At the same time, if I became too powerful, I'd be the one to bring down, because homies may become street famous pursuing a growing star, like the person who killed Billy the Kid in an ambush when the Kid dropped his guard. For all of these reasons, we took our time getting started in the game. We never kept too much money on us at once because it would have made us easy targets for homeboys who hung about the business people. There were a lot of them, believe me.

One was dubbed "Ballhead" and the other "Underdog." Ballhead was the one who worried me the most. He was only 17, a teenager, but he was cruel. I'd never met him before arriving at 81st Street. I learnt quickly. On the street, I observed him jack a number of PCP users. He had no difficulty shoving a pistol or a sawed-off shotgun in the face of someone for $15, $10, or even $5. I imagined him doing the same to me, putting me in a difficult situation. I'd known Underdog since elementary school. He'd spent time in juvenile hall since then, which had hardened him.

Furthermore, not only the conventional dealers, but also the old-school crips, were hooking them up with sherm sticks and beer, which served two functions. It did two things: it kept them at bay, and it put Ballhead and Underdog in a position to repay the favors. It was merely a cost of doing business, similar to a street tax. My strongest defense, though, was that no one knew I was generating money, at least not on 81st Street. A few of the homies who sold PCP began to think that I was doing well in the game, though no one knew for sure because I kept business dealings as discreet as possible.

Money was made on 81st before vice became popular. The odd thing was that when cops finally showed up there, they were looking for PCP, not cocaine. We were ahead of the curve in terms of electricity. And it was relatively simple to defeat them. I, for one, could stand on the block all day without fear of being caught. I only kept a few rocks in my pocket at a time, which I could easily swallow. Furthermore, vice cops were rushing and missing pebbles since there were so many people lined up for pat downs. I had to sell PCP at one time. Ollie and I were running low on cash, so we'd go out at night and put down a car lick on occasion. Keith had become a partner and mentor by that point. He'd tried selling cocaine before, but it didn't work out since he smoked through his entire supply. He had little trouble, though, selling PCP to keep himself afloat.

One night, I felt secure enough to leave my drugs and cash with Keith while Ollie and I went to work to find a car to sell. We rode for at least four hours around the Valley without finding an easy lick. Keith handed me $125 outside, but he owed me $1,400, or a chunk of that in cash and the rest in cocaine. He stated he put the remaining half-ounce on credit. My first lesson was not to leave a parcel with a smoker. I paused for a moment and realized I still needed him. He was more knowledgeable about the drug trade and had more experience than I could have gained on my own. I had to keep him and his expertise close at hand. Nonetheless, as he began to suggest that he'd work off the loan, I cut him off. I didn't have anything left for him to use to pay off his debt. Ollie and I cuddled together. We were back to square one and broke. We only had $125 on hand, and an eight-track (or three grams) would set us back $375. An eight-track would most likely be half-cut, which means it would only be 50% pure. If we didn't take any shorts, we could make roughly $1,100. We agreed to have a decent night's sleep and then restart in the morning.

As soon as we woke up the next morning, I had a plan: to go back into the drug business. I mean selling PCP with Keith as the runner when I say dip. Keith was a smooth talker with established clients, so that would relieve some of our worries. We took $100 of our last $125 to Waterman Tone, the neighborhood's leading PCP supplier. Tone was someone I'd met before; he used to hang around on the street. He had all the gold necklaces and rings, automobiles, cribs, and females we were looking for. He was aware that I sold cocaine, but he saw no future in it. In fact, almost everyone believed the same thing. What he didn't realize was that I had no intention of working for him. I had no chance of competing with him in PCP sales. Fortunately, I didn't want or need to. I'd already thought out how we were going to make money. We could make $600 with a half-ounce of PCP. Then we could purchase an eight-track and go back into the cocaine business.

I'd never used PCP before and had no intention of doing so. I'd seen a lot of people smoking it and selling it, but I had no idea how it got dipped into a bottle. Because I knew many of the customers, I was able to move quickly. My PCP moved quickly. Keith eventually emerged from his long snooze. I accidentally smoked a cigarette, and my world began to spin and twist. I got down on one knee, and that was the end of my day. Ollie, Keith, and I returned to our crib. I relaxed, promising to never use PCP again, and they got to work.

During the process, I learnt an important lesson the hard way: never give someone my entire sack. I had to be prepared to lose my sack if I let someone hold it. Our business took off after we bought our eight-track, or so I thought at the time. I was making between $300 and $400 every day and was content. I had no idea I could make so much more. We once ran into a circumstance in which we couldn't receive narcotics from Mr. Foster or Mike. Ollie had an old flame whose mother, Doris, ran a smokehouse. We went to see Doris, check out her operation, and see if we might buy something from her. That was a brilliant idea. When we arrived at her residence, it was in utter disarray. It appeared that it had not been cleaned in months. The residence did have a large number of people, perhaps 15 or 20, inside doing coke. She was extremely skinny, resembling a skeleton wrapped in skin. Doris was heavier a few years ago, and I recalled her. Her hair looked like it hadn't been brushed in weeks. I only had to give her $50. She motioned for us to take a seat while she went to the back of the home. She returned with the eight-track and some extras she'd bought with her profit. Then she prepared her dish and gently served everyone of us a bite. I said no.

I didn't sneeze. Aside from my introduction to two lines of cocaine with Mike and Ollie during my introduction to the powder, the most I'd ever gotten high on was maybe a drink of beer. It wasn't my cup of tea. At this particular time, I caved and tried it. I felt guilty after leaving her place. I'd learnt not to use it from all the players, from auto thieves to pimps. When you're high, you smoke, snort, or shoot all your profits, and you're just another junkie. Furthermore, you never know when it has been tainted with something else. After that day, I swore myself that I would not do it no matter who asked.

Everyone wanted to chat to me as Keith and I walked back to 81st Street. I was growing into a "Man." They stepped back after a short glance at my face. They could tell I was thinking about something serious. I entered the apartment Ollie was in. Cocaine had permeated the air. Ollie was hiding out in the back bedroom. When I stepped in, a girl got up and began re-putting on her clothing. Something was awry, Ollie realized. Keith accompanied us to Evita's residence, where I confronted Ollie about his smoking. He disputed it at first, but then changed his mind and tried to convince me that he wasn't addicted. Ollie was enraged. Keith had ratted him out, he knew. Keith was grabbed by him. I intervened and broke them up. I handed Keith fifty dollars and sent him on his way. I assured Ollie that we could still collaborate. Despite my reservations, I wanted to give him another chance, especially because we were about to purchase our first half-ounce. We'd saved $1,400, which I'd never thought possible.

We drove to 104th and Buntline and parked in front of Will, Richard's contact's blue house. Will appeared to be in good financial standing. In the fenced-in driveway, at least three Cadillacs with Zeniths were parked. Zenith wheels cost around $3,000 at the time. In addition, a Mercedes-Benz 450SEL 6.9 sat in the driveway. As I passed through the gate, I thought to myself, "These people are wealthy." Richard requested that I give him the money so that he may go in and cop. I never liked hanging up my money to anyone. I immediately remembered Keith's episode. But I recognized Richard. We had a long history together. We used to be friends, and he even stayed with me in my mother's garage for a few weeks. He was an accomplished auto thief who taught me a great deal. I used to enjoy hanging out with him. He also loved to be the boss, which didn't matter when we were stealing automobiles. But I soon discovered that he had the same attitude toward drugs. I wasn't sure if he smoked cocaine or not, but he knew what Ollie would do to him if he tried to beat us up. After all, we were right outside the home in our car. We handed him the cash, and he went inside.

We were riding in a '68 Chevy, a stolen recovery that I'd purchased for a hundred dollars from the police impound yard. The front seat was an odd fit, with the sides bashed in. In addition, the ignition was taken off, so I had to connect two wires to start it. Aside from that, it operated like it was brand new. This made me happy. Everything must have gone well. But he hadn't given me my suitcase yet. We wanted a place to pull over and look it over. Richard stated that his girlfriend stayed down the street. When we arrived, she was standing in the front yard. Rich took out our sack once we were inside. It was a lot of powder, but it didn't come back exactly when we started rocking it up. When I objected, Richard gave me a foolish look until he noticed the seriousness in our looks. So he said that his source, Will, owed him drugs and that he had given him the package. He promised to make things right with us based on that bundle. He took another baggie out of his other pant leg. This appeared to be our belongings as well.

He picked up the phone and made what appeared to be a phony phone call. He hung up and said Will had just departed, but we could change it out later that night. I was skeptical, but I had no choice but to comply. We kept conversing with Penny, catching up, and then we left, leaving Richard at her place. Richard didn't answer his pager at 11 p.m. that night, when he was supposed to meet us. Ollie and I set out to find him. We went to Main Street Mafias, one of Richard's favorite hangouts, then back to Penny's—everywhere we suspected he might be. Nobody had noticed him. Ollie was carrying his pistol, and we were both enraged. We arrived at Manchester Park at 1:30 p.m. Stephan and Fast Eddie were also present. These were massive men. Stephan, also known as "Big Petey" and "Shiesty Petey," and Eddie, also known as "Fast Eddie," appeared to have just gotten out of the pen.

We informed them about Richard robbing us of our money and the house with the Caddies and Benz parked in the driveway. Each of those automobiles had easily two or three grand in accessories. Stephan and Eddie were pleased to help, but knowing there would be a come-up in exchange for their assistance, they requested time to run home and get their gats. This wasn't your average auto theft. It was the kind where guns were pointed at a house's front door and whoever came out got it. It was one thing to steal automobiles. It was another thing entirely to steal from gangsters with a lot of weapons. Cars like the ones those individuals drove were frequently carjacked at stoplights, at gunpoint, and in broad daylight. Cars like those were not driven into South Central by just anyone. It was doubly risky to be in the South Bay neighborhood of Lennox. The sheriff's deputies on patrol in the vicinity were not amused. They were tough. Furthermore, homies responded by stealing their vehicles. I'd heard numerous stories about it. All of this and more ran through my mind as we drove. They weren't the ones that messed me up, but I knew it was Richard. But they were well aware of it when it occurred. They had the funds to repay me. We pulled into 105th in the middle of the night around 2:30 a.m. to nothing but silence. We struck gold when we discovered an alley behind the property. We parked and then strolled two-by-two from opposite sides of the alley. Except for me, everyone else was packing.

The goal was for me to disarm the Caddy's alarm before starting the car. I'd done it numerous times before. This, on the other hand, was most likely the most perilous mission I'd ever been on. I was aware of it at the time. The mansion, the cars, and the surroundings all told me. I started it as soon as we got into the alley, and we were off. We weren't out of there yet, Scott, since deputies pulled over everything that moved at 3 a.m., especially young black men in a nice car. We returned, gathered our belongings, and returned to South Central. We went back to the Westside the next day to sell everything. We didn't want anyone on our side of town knowing what had recently happened. We met Fat Dopie, who owned a Cadillac club. He and his pals bought whatever they could get their hands on. Despite the fact that Zeniths were in high demand, Dopie must have recognized that we were trying to get rid of them quickly since he bargained hard. We decided on $1,400, which was a steal considering these had Vogue tires. Even though the tires were a little worn, we didn't mind because $1,400 was a reasonable price. We still needed to sell the roof, bumper kit, and radio. Those were standard-issue prices. Dopie grabbed his Motorola phone and began spreading the word about what we were selling. Guys approached us and flung money at us before we realized it.

We picked up Fast Eddie and Shiesty Pete on our way home since it was time to split the cash. They weren't going to get very far. Their responsibilities were minor, consisting of keeping watch and moving the car out of the yard. We went to my mother's place as a group of four. They inquired after we split the money, "When are you going to re-up?" about acquiring more dope. As Ollie and I were walking out of the garage, all hell broke loose! A hail of bullets whizzed past us. We looked up and saw three guys blazing away with fully automatic Uzis and Mac-10s. My mother's Cadillac happened to be parked out front, and it served as cover. It was the only thing that kept us from certain death and mayhem. Sirens wailed everywhere, and we retreated. A helicopter buzzed overhead as police encircled my house. Cops had already ordered us to the ground a few homes away from my mother's house. Then they started asking us questions. Meanwhile, we could see just to the end of the tunnel beneath the motorway, where the snipers had ambushed us. We couldn't see what was going on at the other end of the tunnel, but we did learn that Richard, the snitch, was also one of the guns. My heart was still racing against my chest when I returned to my house, where authorities were interviewing my mother in the front yard, with everyone around her car.

I knew they assumed the whole thing was drug-related from the start of the interrogation, but we all kept quiet and stated we had no idea what the shooting was about. But I felt they were too strong for us and had far too much firepower. Imagine what they'd do if we tried to hit one of them if they shot up the neighborhood over a car. The cops had officially designated me as the commander of the Freeway Boys by this point. I informed the boys that we needed to take it easy for a bit to see what else, if anything, happened. Meanwhile, we needed to gather our money and weaponry.It turned out to be advantageous. The 81st Street location became a secure haven for me. In the 'hood, I was starting to be treated like a celebrity. Everyone knew who I was. I did everything I could to keep an eye on my homies, and they did the same for me. Nobody dared to touch me while I was on 81st.

I started to feel safe again a few days after the shooting at my mother's house, especially with Ollie armed and by my side. I ran into Moomoo around that time. He and I had both attended Bret Harte in seventh grade. Early in the game, we worked the streets together. Moomoo has a near-legendary reputation. He was a founding member of the 107 Hoover Crips. We embraced like brothers when we saw each other. Things proceeded swimmingly for the next two months. The grind was constant, 24 hours a day, seven days a week. We were doing $3,000 to $4,000 each day on 81st. I could see the operation generating $10,000 each day. The homies, though, continued to discuss vengeance against Richard and Will. Having Moomoo on my team made it simpler, but I was thinking about those $10,000 days, trying to block out anything that didn't result in a profit, even though I knew it wasn't over with Richard and Will. I was grabbing lunch at Taco Pete's when I ran across One-eyed Kenny, whom I knew from my low-riding days. But because his brother lived across the street from Will, I wasn't sure whose side he'd be on. When we started talking about the incident, I was wary. The meeting's rules were then established. We couldn't bring more than two guys, and no weapons of any type were permitted. Melvin would make certain that his environment was secure and that the rules were obeyed.

I brought Donnie and Ollie with me as backup since I knew how they'd react under pressure if something went wrong. If there was going to be violence, Donnie would run into it rather than away from it. He had no fear. I wasn't sure who Will would bring, but I knew it wouldn't be Richard, who was still in the L.A. County jail. We arrived at Melvin's garage for the rendezvous. Will clarified himself. He said that the shooting was entirely Richard's idea, and that he was not present when Richard made the decision to retaliate for Will's car being stolen. I had some faith in him, but I couldn't help but be cautious. Then I considered what motivated him, and it persuaded me. I knew it was all about money and his business, and that was exactly what drove me. Furthermore, he was perhaps the wealthiest man in South Central at the time, with a lot to lose. He claimed it was over, and we didn't have to worry about anything. I agreed since he wanted to pay for the damage to my mother's car. He even offered to sell us medicines to help us back on our feet. I thanked him and said I'd think about it. I was still hoping to believe him. I was even relieved that he was being honest with me. But getting into the coke industry with this guy was a very different story. We shook hands after that. At the very least, the bad blood was behind us.

# CHAPTER 12
# BLOODS 'N TURF

We were back on 81st Street, and there was no shortage of customers. I was a young man coming into my own at the time. Sharon, my Belizean girlfriend, was still with me. She was finishing high school, and her mother was strict, so I could only see her once or twice a week. She was where my heart was, and she was involved in the cocaine trade. Getting to Sharon, on the other hand, was a challenge. It was difficult to find time to spend with her, especially when she was alone. Women I knew began to treat me as if I were the catch of the century. It's amazing what money and power can do. My main concern was obtaining a consistent supply of medications. My game was open 24 hours a day, seven days a week from the start. Nothing, not even ladies looking to trade sex for cocaine, could stand in the way of that.

I began speaking with prominent people who had the power to make things happen. I got in touch with Buddy, one of my old car-thief buddies. I'd always gotten along well with Buddy. His younger brother, Big Mike, who owned a slew of booze stores, had worked with me a few years before. Buddy was informed of my predicament. He claimed that he could handle it since he knew people in high places. I told him how much money I had at the time, approximately $6,000 to invest. Nonetheless, I had entire faith in Buddy. He'd never played any games with me before. Everything had always been on the straight and narrow. He knew I was serious if I said it. I informed him about my spot and painted a mental picture of how it was jumping in his head. I was on my way up, so I probably told him that as well. He gave me a note with his address on it. Because I couldn't read at the time, I gave the note to Ollie. Buddy, he said, stayed in Palisades. I was blown away. We competed in tennis versus Palisades High. I had a feeling the neighborhood would be lovely.

I'd never drunk much before, but I sipped a margarita while we sat and waited for the medications. Buddy stated that he would charge us $2,800 per ounce. We watched his cable television, which was novel to us. We'd been there for almost an hour when Big Mike, Buddy's partner, walked in with a bag. I told him the narrative, knowing he was Buddy's partner, and then he counted out the money, and Ollie and I seized custody of the drugs. We returned and checked on the medications, and everything was fine. We preferred doing business with Mr. Foster. The issue with Foster was that he was untrustworthy. He was up for the sell some days and didn't feel like it others. That is not how I would manage a business. Now that we had Jonny Mumbles, he would hold the narcotics and sell them, while I would hold the gun and collect them. We also rented apartments and houses from others. We'd make arrangements with them for a $50 rock to set up and sell in their homes. It always costs more than that, believe me.

I went down to see an old friend who ran an auto mechanic business on 66th and Vermont. I used to do a few things for him. Before I was raided, our stores were just next to each other. Lloyd was quite the character. He had Don King's hair before Don King became famous. He previously worked as a writer for black comedian Rudy Ray Moore. We tallied the rocks—two made from Buddy's two ounces—and bagged over $15,000 worth. We may earn up to $4,000 every day. I intended to return to him and request that he schedule it as soon as possible. I couldn't possibly have enough. We never stopped looking for sources; it was an unending search. When I was at Mr. Foster's, I asked for a quarter pound. He dialed Mark, his middleman above Foster. Then Mark called Ivan, a guy higher up. Ivan advised him that the transaction could be completed in three hours. The transaction price was fixed at $2,400 per ounce. We reduced our sale price yet again. Ollie and I weren't swindling the pricing because we were simply concerned with consistency. People on 81st Street were aware of the money being made from cocaine transactions.

At the time, an eight-track cost between $375 and $400 and weighed 3.5 grams. But Ollie and I discovered that when we bought a modest quantity, it had most likely been walked on so hard that it was only one gram of genuine coke. We were able to transport three grams of clean, high-quality goods. The dealers had never seen anything like that before and had no idea what good coke was. We began selling eight-track tapes to hustlers. We could get a little more than nine recordings out of one ounce. We made $3,300 on a $2,400 investment with far less work than before. Business was booming. Instead of just being street dealers, we'd become distributors.

Then an idea struck me. I needed a couple more collaborators. I needed to broaden my horizons. One route was through Ramon, who was known as the "King of the Weed." Ramon exploited Fourth and Main for pot sales in the same manner that 81st specialized in PCP. It was similar to a drive-up supermarket. I'd seen them sell so many $20 bags that it wasn't even funny. I knew smoking cocaine may knock people out. I'd seen folks in those smoke houses who were previously affluent and famous slide from coke addiction, so I devised a strategy for my homeboys to escape it. I had to first inform them they were addicted, that they were junkies. They couldn't get away from it. I wanted to force them to leave just to prove me wrong. It was successful. They resigned. Ramon was constantly trying to outdo me. It was like a competition for him to go off narcotics. I informed them how many ounces I was going to buy. Ramon stated he could match my purchase if we both bought. So we struck a bargain. It was not a problem for me. I was well aware that the more I purchased, the cheaper it would get.

Rich Ronnie was another homeboy I hooked up with. I first encountered Ronnie when Ollie, Jeff, and I attempted to steal his car.

I was still new to the streets, low-riding, and fresh off the tennis courts back then. Ronnie's car was a gorgeous blue-and-white Cutlass with all the bells and whistles. People have been killed because of his Big Hub rims. They were absolute classics. We were desperate for some. Whim stayed on 84th Street and Ronnie stayed on 88th Place. I saw the automobile as soon as we arrived at Ronnie's house and knew who I'd be meeting. But I doubted he'd remember me because so much had changed in that year and a half. I was broke and chasing his car the last time he saw me. He was undoubtedly one of the wealthiest black guys in South Central by this point. Whim was in the lead, but Ronnie was the first to acknowledge me. Ronnie recognized me, which shocked me because I wasn't the only one there that night. Then he opened the door for us. Inside was a platter with rock cocaine, powder cocaine, marijuana, and cigarettes. Ronnie informed me that he had been selling cannabis and PCP. Now I understand how he got his car to fly so high. Ronnie was an astute negotiator. He was said to have done some pimpin' in his day. He knew his way around town. We settled on $1,800 per ounce. He'd purchase two, and I'd put up two. It had been decided. We exchanged handshakes, and I promised to return in less than 30 minutes.

Next on my agenda of networking activities to attract another partner was a trip to Nickerson Gardens. It was a risk. The Nickersons were full of Bloods. Tyrone was the only person I knew from the Nickersons. I hadn't seen him in a few months, but I needed to speak with him right away. Tyrone was selling "water," which was the street name for PCP. He also performed admirably. I made my way to Nickerson Gardens, a public housing project with over a thousand apartments. Tyrone was a resident of one of them. Guys on the sidewalk near Tyrone's building could tell I wasn't from there when I stepped out of the car. They began to "Blood" me, but I was confident I could get to Tyrone's place before anything bad happened. The tone shifted when they noticed me heading toward his door. They backed off when I knocked. Tyrone was my senior.

Because his younger brother was a Freeway Boy, he regarded me as a homeboy. I told him about my drug venture inside the flat. He laughed. He replied he'd heard about cocaine but hadn't tried it yet. I urged him to accompany me to 81st and see for himself how much money was being produced there.

It was a 180-degree turn from how I was treated when I came into the projects with Tyrone. So that's what it's like to be with someone who is well-liked by everyone, I reasoned. I was picking up new skills quickly. When we arrived at 81st, I directed him to where Ollie and Mumbles were waiting for us. Tyrone and Mumbles were great. Tyrone's younger brother and Mumbles had smoked PCP together. My crew's other members have tried it a few times as well. Cruz Dog was another. I don't know if Ollie ever smoked. I know a few of my other guys did. When they did it, I was harsh on all of them. I wanted them to stay focused on selling. I was never given a position of authority. It was just something I ended up doing. The boys respected me for it.

There were around 40 apartments in the neighborhood, divided into two rows. The first was pink, and the second was lime green. This was prior to the city's installation of barbed-wire fences and closed gates to keep people out. Perhaps the gates were there to keep people in. It was often impossible to identify which direction it was meant. We talked as we walked down the street. Tyrone was a foregone conclusion in my mind. He informed me that he had all the funds necessary to put up a deal straight now. As I drove back from dropping him off, I reflected on how great things were going. I felt like an entrepreneur starting a company. I sped back to Ollie to deliver him the new deal. When I returned to Ollie, we said, in our usual tone, "Nigga, we fixin' to be on top." I persuaded him to take a break and accompany me to M&M Soul Food for lunch.

At the table, Ollie and I made preparations to close our deal that night. It'd be the most dope we'd ever seen in one location. Situations like that can be exciting, but in a positive manner. There wasn't much to do in terms of preparation other than pray for the best. When a certain deal is your first time, it plays with your anxieties as you go up the drug game ladder. The more you do it, the more comfortable you will become. The apprehension of dealing with such a vast quantity faded with each transaction. We weren't going to earn a profit on the first deal. It hadn't yet dawned on us that the more we bought, the cheaper items were, especially in terms of ounces. We also had a variety of suppliers, some of whom gave us better costs. Not that the quality was as outstanding, but it made me think that we should deliberately seek lower prices.

When we got to Foster's house, Ollie and I went inside to complete the transaction. Foster called his contact Ivan and his brother-in-law, Henry. They had to be nearby because they arrived at Mr. Foster's in less than five minutes. We sat in the living room and placed the money—roughly $45,000—on a coffee table. It equated to nearly $2,800 every 16 ounces. We didn't know how to count money back then. Money was everywhere in my house because we didn't separate the different bills; instead, we piled hundreds of them together. We exchanged handshakes with Ivan and Henry. On both sides, there was cautious suspicion. We couldn't interact with them because we had to obey the chain of command. This was before we discovered Mr. Foster had been smoked out.

It was a massive lump of rock in a large Ziploc bag, with a little shaking. Mr. Foster received the suitcase from Henry. We all exchanged nods before Henry and Ivan stepped out the door. Mr. Foster put a piece of paper inside the bag after they departed and drew out the shake, which was about an eighth of an ounce. That was his contribution to the arrangement. Seven grams may not seem like much, but Ollie and I could make $300 each gram. Even though Mr.

Foster put us through hell because he was wishy-washy, it was all part of the job. He was still offering the greatest deal in town. We grabbed the bag and rolled out. We climbed into the van and handed the bag back to Tyrone and Ramon to investigate. They examined it, but they trusted our judgment. The purchase had already been approved, so we returned to my mother's garage, where Tyrone and Ramon had left their automobiles. It was our old hangout, and we now kept a triple-beam scale there. It was a place to unwind and unwind. While we took care of business, I requested my cousin Kenny and Cruz to stand guard. We went into the garage and weighed everyone's belongings. We divided the bag into three equal halves and placed them in Baggies. Tyrone and Ramon then continued on their journey. In my opinion, I'd just delivered drugs to a new dealer at Nickersons on Main Street.

We were growing so quickly that we couldn't believe it. Ollie didn't normally talk to people, so I was the one who had to answer all the inquiries. I informed everyone that we'd yell at them in a few minutes. I promised Ollie I'd yell at him as he made his way up the stairs. I could tell that the block was doing nicely. However, when we arrived upstairs, where Mumbles was waiting, there was money all over the place. Ollie appeared to be shaking him down. Money might be found in every pocket, sock, shoe, and orifice. I wasn't sure how much marijuana we had left for Mumbles, but he'd sold it all. Every crumb. He was hungry for more. 81st had transitioned from a sherm track to a cocaine track by this point. Nobody sold PCP anymore, and it became scarce. I recall the look on Waterman Tone's face when the switch was made and I took over his track. It took him a couple of months to realize what was going on. He approached me and asked if I could put him down. This happened frequently. Guys I believed were better than me were becoming my employees. On 81st Street, there was plenty of money for everyone, so I set them down. A few days before the first of the month, almost all of the mothers in the apartment complex inquired about investing their welfare checks.

Because so many of them expressed interest, it appeared to be a well-organized scheme. Welfare payments for coke. Because I had so many prepaid customers, I knew it was going to be my busiest day ever. My network was expanding.

Ramon called because a young woman wanted to buy a quarter-ounce of marijuana. He would not sell it to her. She demanded $700 for it. We were still able to make $300 to $325 off of one gram. If he sold it for that, he'd be working at a loss. I'd previously figured out how to sell in bulk. Ramon arranged the rendezvous with Ingrid, the young lady known as Goldie, or Red Goldie. She had an apartment on 96th Street that backed up to the back of M&M's. Her car simply blended in with the restaurant's traffic. Ingrid had an out-of-this-world figure that was also quite attractive. The disadvantage was that she was a mobster at heart and had a reputation for doing a lot of gangster stuff. I'd heard of her but had never met her. We got her going. I sold her the seven grams, and she paid in new $100 bills. I considered hitting, but I was concerned that it would interfere with the money. I was particularly interested in her. Because she had no ego, that was the start of our relationship. Our friendship blossomed. I believe she returned the next day and purchased an ounce. I would give her one on credit whenever she bought one. I just reduced her asking price by a few bucks. She brought her two sisters with her the following time she came. Ingrid had become my most important customer, and our friendship was blossoming. She and Ollie became involved, which was fine with me because whatever Ingrid desired, she got.

I was up to $200,000 and $300,000 by then, and I could do whatever I wanted, whenever I wanted. One day when we had nothing to do, a few of us hung together. Someone advised us to visit Magic Mountain. We went to Magic Mountain and had a fantastic time. Money did not exist. We participated in all of the games, ate, and drank. I was on the hunt for Robbin, one of Ingrid's friends. She was stunning, and she worked at Baskin-Robbins. I bought a lot of ice cream during the next few weeks. After a day at Magic Mountain, it was back to work the next day. We had so much money that we didn't even bother counting it. We'd just count enough to replenish our supplies. A pound costs around $32,000, or $2,000 per ounce. It was a wonderful deal for us. Ingrid bought one ounce a day on top of what I paid her. Ramon and Tyrone came over every day to get quarter-pounds, which we sold for $450 each.

We kept our hoard in my mother's house and my old bedroom. We stuffed the cash into the back closet and covered it with old garments. We'd long given up on utilizing shoeboxes because there weren't enough of them. My mother had kicked me out of the house. Because of all the travels we took, I assumed she was aware of what we were up to. I was certain she suspected me of drug use. I'd sold the vehicle accessories to buy narcotics, but not for myself. I believed it was a waste of money to have $6,000 in garish decorations on my automobile when that same $6,000 might make me $1,200. Mom was like a den mother to all the boys. They slept and ate at her place, and my mother expected them to be respectful. She instructed me to go grab Ollie and Mumbles. I could see we were in big trouble.

That was supposed to be the day we left. We had originally planned to make $5,000. We couldn't even buy gas before we started the game. We were impoverished. But it was too late. There was no turning back now. Mom gave us a religious speech about acquiring and losing your soul after we tallied and stacked the money. She begged and pleaded with us that if we were in the crowd and had a way out, now was the time. I adored my mother and despised seeing her in this state. I attempted to inform her politely and truthfully that we were going to leave soon. I couldn't guarantee her a date, and I had no intention of quitting anytime soon. I'd finally found my calling. I was proving those who thought I'd never amount to anything wrong. I was a significant figure in the city with $100,000 in cash after only six or seven months.

I went to see my old friend Monk once I had finished talking to everyone. He was one of the primary Street Mafia's shot callers, if not the primary man. He sold a couple dime bags of marijuana and worked at the alternator shop on 98th and Main. I knew he'd be a terrific ally, just like Ramon and Tyree. Who'd have guessed? Perhaps even better. When I arrived at 98th and Main, the guys were standing outside. T.C., Fish, Psycho Mike, Baby Boy, Little Monk, and a few unknown cats. Because they knew Monk and I were homies, I already had love on Main Street. When I called his name, he poked his head out the garage door of the generator shop. Monk was a few years younger than me, and he always referred to me as O.G. I stepped over to the door and we exchanged high fives.

When I returned to 81st Street, there were cops everywhere. But I recognized it wasn't a standard raid because the cars were black-and-whites and a couple of Metros, not the type of automobiles that were typical of drug raids. When I pulled up and saw Ollie and Mumbles standing near the roadway, I knew they wouldn't be detained. I strolled back toward Ollie and Mumbles after parking the car down the street. We did not sell drugs from her home. It served as both a cache location and a place for us to sleep. We observed that our supply was running low. Evita had my complete regard and trust. She was my favorite female cousin and taught me a lot about business. Her daughters were like my children, and since I didn't have any at the time, it was personal for me. We'd smoked primos before, but it was meant to be a one-time occurrence. It was just another experiment for me. I eventually discovered that Evita had not quit—and had no intention of doing so. To say the least, things were bumpy at our location. When she was released from jail, she raised hell and made a lot of noise. "Why did it take you so long to get me out?" she wondered.

After bailing her out, I met with Monk that same evening. I rolled back to 98th and Main. This time I took an eight-track with me. It was my gift to Monk. It was a wise investment. He had a crew of about 50 under him and that meant I would be able to put the product out that much more efficiently. He had a homegirl who stayed on the corner of 98th. Her name was Louise, even though I didn't know it at the time. We headed into the kitchen and I cooked up the coke for him. I showed him how to add the baking soda, how to put it into a pot of boiling water and watch it turn to gel. Add some cold water, shake gently, and it forms into one big rock. Once it turned hard, we took it out of the shaker bottle. Then I started to cut it up for him. I cut him $1,100 worth. I told him all he had to do was offer it to all of his marijuana customers and it would start to move. I could see the skeptical look in his eye. I'd seen that same look many times before. He knew I'd never lied to him before.

Monk was not your everyday, average thug. He'd been in jail for shooting at cops, for manslaughter, and, I'd heard, for rape. He couldn't have been much older than 18. He was big; he'd been hitting the iron hard. He commanded respect throughout the various 'hoods. As I walked out the door, I thought to myself, What a move I just made. Because Monk's place wasn't far from where Ingrid stayed on 96th and Avalon, I decided to swing by and pay her a visit. And, man, was she doing. When I walked up to the door, she recognized me, and, with pistol in hand, she opened the door. Her coffee table was covered with money. Some little skinny kid in the house was with her. He had a Jerry curl and I could tell he was a pretty boy. She ordered him to the back bedroom when I walked in. I wasn't trippin' about it, because she wasn't my woman. She told me she wanted to buy 16 ounces. I'd never sold 16 ounces to anyone. My biggest two guys were Ramon and Tyree, and she just went past them even though I hadn't been working with her for more than a month and a half. I explained that it was cool and I'd set it up. I didn't quote her a price right off the bat; I needed time to consider it. Plus, I wanted to run it by Ollie and see what he thought.

Ollie and I finished discussing Ingrid's deal. We were buying two to three pounds at a time and getting them for around $2,100 an ounce. This Ingrid deal was going to be our biggest single transaction. It made me wonder about Tyree and Ramon. Why weren't they buying bigger quantities? I made a point of going by Ramon's spot. He had a brand new Maroon Cadillac, a Fleetwood Brougham with all the fixin's, sitting out front. He paid $16,000 for it. His traffic was so heavy, he was buying quarter pounds just about every day. On my way back, I ran into Little Pete. He was from Watts and ran with the Grape Street Crips. He was a low ranker, but he was somebody I'd always had respect for. I heard he was in the water game. He had some cars too. I saw him at the gas station and we talked. I'd learned a valuable lesson on 81st Street: PCP guys and weed guys could all be converted. It's the old saying, "Go with the highest bidder." Cocaine had become the new king. Pete started with a quarter-pound that same day. His watering days were over. I gave him a deal, $2,600 an ounce, and I knew he'd gotten the best stuff he'd ever had.

When Pete went to get his quarter, he brought Albert Griffin, also known as Benzo Al, with him. Al was also a fan of water. And he drove one of the coolest Cadillacs in town. In the beginning, Ollie and I went to Albert to obtain some PCP. I showed Pete how to make the coke. It was done in my mother's garage. Everyone knew where that location was, and it had become safe. We'd gotten out of the car-stealing business because it was too dangerous. We finished with Pete, who was yet another satisfied customer. I was also aware that we had Benzo Al. I could see he was sold by the look on his face. But I knew it wasn't proper for Dad to crack on me in front of Pete. Later that day, I'd make myself available to him.

There was also Little Tommy. He used to be a member of my low-rider club. He was about 14 years old when I first met him. He drove the ugliest '63 Chevy I'd ever seen. But one thing struck me about him: his determination. Tommy was already out of the loop. I observed the bright orange '63 Chevy parked in the driveway on one of my visits to my mother's house. The automobile appeared to have been painted with a paintbrush. I was relieved to see him because he reminded me of one of my younger brothers.

I was establishing my future rivals while I was building an empire of employees and managers for the street to move the cocaine. When everyone becomes wealthy and successful, they may decide that working for someone else, such as myself, is no longer economically viable. Then they'll rebel and try to take control of the game. That's what happened to several of my employees eventually. After Tommy told me what he'd been up to, I promised him to come back later that night and I'd hook him up. I already had too much dope to sell, so I was looking for others to sell it for me. I gave him a half-ounce later that night. I told him he'd have to bring me $1,400 back. He had no idea what I was talking about, but I told him he should be able to make at least $3,000 off of it. He was beaming from ear to ear. I knew he'd be satisfied with what I offered him because Ramon didn't care about anyone but himself. We completed the trade, and Tommy returned the next day with $2,800. This time, I fed him two ounces. One was paid in full and one was paid in advance. I wanted to reduce the number of transactions I was performing. First and foremost, safety. I also let Tommy know where he could find me on 81st Street if he needed me. The next time I saw Tommy, he directed me to his 82nd Street location. That was odd because he hadn't had a spot on 82nd for several weeks. I merely shook my head as I walked into the house. He was taking all of our leftovers, as well as any walk-in business that we might miss. He was drinking from the same well that we were. That was fine with me because I was charging top dollar for ounces of my stuff. I was still oblivious to the danger.

Tommy brought Haney, another of our low-riding buddies, with him on one of those outings. Haney was interested. Tommy was the type to show off his wealth. We couldn't have been coworkers for more than three months before he got his first Mercedes. I guess it worked both ways because a lot of the young boys in the neighborhood would approach me and say they saw Tommy rollin' and wanted to do the same. I was continuously on the lookout for new employees. There was only so much Ollie, Mumbles, and I could do. It was becoming more difficult to keep Ollie and Mumbles on board. That's when I had an inspiration: if I could give Tommy a half-ounce and he did well, why not do it for the entire Freeway crew? I convened a meeting. I planned for the Freeway Boys to meet at Manchester Park because I wanted everyone to attend and it would be too large at my mother's place. There were at least 20 to 40 people, but only 40 ounces—maybe a little more. None of these individuals had previously sold cocaine. I was concerned that some of them may taint the goods, so I laid out the ground rules. There would be no smoking allowed. What I was providing them was theirs to keep and do with as they pleased—another blunder. I informed them that we would be driving traffic from 81st to Denver Street. That was a similarly laid-out neighborhood, but this was our fortress.

Denver also made contact with Manchester Boulevard, which housed the Forum. People started telling me that we had it going so hard that it seemed like a Lakers game was happening every day. He cracked on me after Haney dropped by with Tommy. He stated that he desired to be put down. I really liked him. I felt he'd be useful to the squad. I tossed him two ounces, and he began to roll. It didn't take long for him to start looking like Mr. T. He and Tommy were the first people I ever saw with diamond-encrusted hubcaps on their chests. Haney was accompanied by some of the most beautiful women I'd ever seen, and I was curious as to where they came from. He said he'd meet them at the skating rink. So I suggested, "Let's go to the rink." I had never gone to World on Wheels before. It felt like a candy store. Chicks were all over the place. That was the first time I saw Whitey from Whitey Enterprise. There were around ten of them, each wearing a jacket with the same name on the back. They were at war with the Third World. This was a battle for territory between drug dealers. Haney was getting attention from all sides. You'd swear he was the wealthiest person in the building.

We all rolled out when the night came to an end and the skating rink closed. Ollie and I had recently moved into our first apartment. We spent a little money sprucing up an ancient wooden duplex. The man who rented it to us charged us only $300 per month. We had to leave since the situation with Evita had gotten out of hand. Her mother accused me of introducing my cousin to drugs. Evita defended me. The landlord then arrived, accompanied by a county marshal. We were all evicted because Evita had not been paying the landlord the rent we had paid her. That is how we came to have our own place.

On our way home, I told Marilyn that I needed to stop by my house and collect my car. She was perfectly fine with it. When we arrived at the house and entered, homies were spread all over the place, as if it were a refugee camp or something. People were just hanging out and watching TV. I decided to invite her into my bedroom, away from my friends. It was time for me to strike. What I actually wanted was someone to sleep with. The next day, I returned to Marilyn's house. I'd previously discussed it with Monk. He said the homegirl was cool and didn't get high, and I agreed. She had a lot of potential. We walked in and assembled everything so she could begin rolling. I instructed her to bring me $2,400 on an ounce back. 98th Street soon began to take considerable traffic. Monk and Little Monk were doing an excellent job. The entire neighborhood was now waiting to join in on the fun. I had no idea how eagerly they were anticipating my arrival. Marilyn couldn't have phoned me for more than three or four hours. She had more heart than Monk, or perhaps she felt she could get away with more since she was a woman. Perhaps it was a combination of the two. She was selling in bulk. I was excited to see what she could do. She asked me to meet her at the skating rink, which I gladly did.

When I turned around to fetch a hot dog and a slushie, there was Wayne Day, also known as Honcho. I had last seen him when I drew a revolver on him. Honcho was a bull's strength, comfortably benching 500 pounds. He was accompanied by two children on this particular night. Honcho was the president of the Majestics Car Club and a shot caller for the Grape Street Crips. Some people can hold a grudge for the rest of their lives. Honcho and I have done a few vehicle jobs together before, but I'm quite sure he always looked down on me. But not on that particular night. He presented me with my props. Perhaps my reputation was greater than I anticipated.

I welcomed him into the fold. I also met Chubb, Honcho's first cousin, who had recently been released from the Youth Authority. We began walking around the roller rink together. Honcho told me as we went that he'd heard tales about what I was up to. I asked if he'd started doing cocaine yet. He said he hadn't, but he'd heard it was a profitable venture. We agreed to meet the next day at Ollie's mother's place. He had money before, but not the type of money he was about to get. I escorted him and Chubb to the car, where he stuffed the eight ounces inside his moonroof. I thought to myself, "I just scored a big one." It was incredible to have Honcho on the team. He didn't let me down. Honcho didn't return for another two or three days. He had $45,000 and was ready to take the money. Honcho reigned with a heavy hand. He was the type of person who would not allow anyone to sell drugs in his projects unless it was his own cocaine. He has a team in place to enforce the rules. He was involved in the game and worked for me.

# CHAPTER 13
# WHEELING AND DEALING

People were lining up to be a part of my team. Every week, I enlisted additional dealers, and not just any dealers. There were two in particular that stuck out. Doc Rob was a Bakersfield police officer, and Dee worked for the California Highway Patrol. Ollie and I were close to them because we'd grown up together. We weren't surprised when they arrived and stated they were ready to party. Their street contacts provided them with the opportunity to make a lot of money. We were delighted to have them on board. Then Dean informed me he had a friend, Stacy, at the Pueblo Del Rio housing projects in Watts' Low Bottoms neighborhood. Stacy, he claimed, had the heroin industry figured out and knew how to make money. He wanted me to meet her.

Dean drove me to Pueblo, to the intersection of Holmes Avenue and 54th Street. Kids in the projects drove Mercedes Benzes and Chevy pickups with the tops cut off, all supercharged and decked out. Homies shelled out $5,000 for paint treatments. Everyone seemed to be sporting new low-rider wheels dubbed Daytons, which might cost up to $3,200 per set. Obviously, the young people who were doing so well had to be selling something. The Pueblo Bishop Bloods controlled this territory. Dean wasn't banging, but he was dressed in the Blood color of choice, cherry red. We pulled over and got out of the car as a battle was taking place, in which a girl around 6-foot-1, 200 pounds, and all muscle was whooping on a guy. Without Dean, I would not have gone inside. I still had my 9-millimeter with me. Everyone in the parking lot had firearms on them as well. There had been some recent tension among the homies there, which had resulted in a few drive-by shootings. The cops termed it gang unrest.

As the remodel progressed, the contractor began to add to the house. We spent roughly $150,000 on a house that was probably only $65,000 new. I'd never heard of sod until a truck showed up with pallets of it one day. It was delivered with its own forklift. The same workers that put up the basketball rims in the Forum arena also put up the fiberglass backboards on our court. I was first proud of the house and its upgrades, but I eventually grew wary of the attention it drew. It became difficult as the process continued. We didn't want the house to stand out like a sore thumb. To make matters worse, our soldiers were blowing up overnight. People drove up to the house in Porches, Mercedes Benzes, Rolls Royces, and so on. We were becoming very noticeable.

I couldn't decide whether that was a good or terrible thing. Nonetheless, we felt safe in that property, which was located on the I-10 freeway side of 88th and Grand. We didn't have neighbors on one side, and our friends and families lived across the street and down the block, and many of them came to the house to hang out. That was our way of life for a while. Every day brought a new hook-up, and every week brought a new buyer. The money kept coming in. Then, one day, I paged Ivan, one of our Nicaraguan suppliers, and when he didn't respond, I paged him again. There is still no response. That continued all day, the next day, and for a week. We began to feel desperate.

We'd made a monster. I had an idea where we could find out more about Ivan. We'd met him before with another Nicaraguan, Tony, who ran a modest clothes and manufacturing business. Tony stated he hadn't seen Ivan in months until we arrived. He did, however, offer to connect us. The price was steep: $34,000 per pound, which was little less than what we were selling it for after dividing it up into 16 ounces. However, we agreed to buy two to get things started. We needed coke for our dealers, and we expected the price to fall. Tony made his phone calls, and we set out to fetch the money. When we returned to his shop, he informed us that the transaction would take place at his home. We went there and let him count the money before he called the contact. Another Latino knocked on the door fifteen minutes later. He was carrying a brown bag that appeared to contain two pounds of cocaine. He was also acting paranoid. Tony took the money bag from me and delivered it to the guy, then he took the cocaine bag and passed it to me. I opened the bag and immediately knew it wasn't cocaine. It would most likely make a tasty cake, but it would not get you high. When I looked up, Tony's connection had gone out the door like he was on fire. I sprang up and dashed after him. Ollie chased after me. I observed him get into his car, which was already running. When I arrived at Grump and Zo, who hadn't been paying attention, we started our car and the chase began.

We chased him into downtown Los Angeles before losing him in Washington and Vermont. When we returned to Tony's house, Ollie had already summoned the rest of the homies, who went to his house and severely beat him. Tony immediately agreed to drive us past his friend's place. Tony, without a doubt, had no idea that his link was going to burn us and had nothing to do with the hoax. I drove him home because I knew he was innocent, misled like we were. I didn't want anything to happen to him anymore. Still, Tony was terrified. He offered me everything he owned to ensure that no one else touched him. I reassured him that everything was fine. He walked away from my car, holding the side of his head, but with a much calmer expression on his face. He was clearly relieved and grateful to be alive.

After that, I contacted Buddy. We hadn't communicated in months. I told him how much money I had—roughly $350,000, give or take a few thousand, not including what I was selling on consignment. He set up a meeting with his brother, Big Mike. Mike informed me that his pal, Chinese Dave, had recently been released from prison and was a major coke boy. I spoke with him, and he said he'd start me at

$2,100 per ounce. I didn't enjoy it, but at least we were getting something done. We began with about two or three pounds. He handed me a couple more pounds on the front after we performed a couple of deals. We didn't need it because we have enough money. However, it demonstrated the trust component, which was significant. Although the money was not expanding as quickly as it had previously, it was still growing. Dave must have realized he couldn't keep up with our speed. I was certain I had more money than he did. One day, he mentioned that his dope originated from Miami and that if we traveled there to obtain it, it would be much cheaper. Dave had been in the game for a long time and was well-versed in the cocaine trade. The Nicaraguans had kept us at a safe distance, but Dave had invited us in. We could drive any of his automobiles to his house whenever we wanted. He felt like one of the gang. I felt at ease with him, especially after we'd collaborated on a number of transactions.

We started planning how we'd get the money to Miami. I'd never previously transported drugs out of town. I'd shipped it with my twin cousins to Texas, but it was only four ounces. I'd take four ounces of anything. This time, however, we were talking about over 50 pounds. Dave always had two ounces of snort on him for personal usage. He snorted the entire trip to Miami in our rented four-door Lincoln Continental. In the car, I teased Dave for snorting so much. I stood to lose a lot if this thing blew apart. We arrived in Miami and settled into a motel near the airport while waiting for a call. When we returned, Ollie ordered pizza and I went to confront Dave. When I arrived in his room, he was doing what he did best: snorting powder up his nose while talking on the phone. Nevel sat back and watched TV. I didn't play with Nevel much. He'd appeared on the scene, and Dave had given him the job of right-hand guy. I was slightly envious. We had it out the first time Dave took him to my house. Nevel was a black man who appeared white. When I initially saw him, I assumed he was a cop.

Dave stated that everything was scheduled for the following day. I was relieved because I had no idea what was going on in the neighborhood. We left the motel the next day to settle the score. I became worried when I arrived at the spot, a two-story apartment complex. I've heard a variety of stories. We were strapless down there. Dave refused to bring the entire sum until we viewed the product. He was an expert at this, so I followed in his footsteps. The score was lowered without incident. I got 20 keys, whereas Chinese Dave got 12. We left for Georgia, our first stop. Chinese Dave had the brilliant notion of driving with Florida plates until we got out of the state and then switching cars. We rode along the highway, four of us, with 32 keys placed like bricks in front of us. One of the ounces exploded, scattering dust everywhere. I honestly believed there was no chance this could end well.

I was relieved when we parked into a Georgia hotel for the night. I dialed California right away. The guys stated they'd be going out to Indiana in a motor home to meet us. If we made it home with the cocaine, it would be a big score. We went automobile shopping the next morning. Dave chose a '83 Toyota van that was fully stocked. It resembled a breadbox. It had tinted windows and was anything but noticeable. The journey would unquestionably be more comfortable than in the Lincoln. Dave had promised to pay the van in cash for $28,000. We went to a few banks, obtained a cashier's check, and I drove that sucker off the lot. We drove another 12 hours to Indianapolis, where we met up with the homies. We hid the pills in the motorhome's ceiling. From then on, everything went swimmingly. There are no cops. No worries.

# CHAPTER 14
# MIAMI OR BUST

When we returned to Los Angeles, Dave demanded that I give him a kilo of drugs in exchange for the van, a deceptive maneuver that cost me at least $10,000. I could have sold the key, paid him for the van, and still made a five-figure profit. Then he demanded another kilo for connecting me to the connection, claiming that he had not included any "taxes" in the fee. I was enraged, but I realized that this was how the game frequently played out—all part of the game of moving cocaine. I ended up with 18 keys instead of my initial 20. In addition, the van was a thoughtful gift for my mother. It's similar to making lemonade from lemons. I could still make close to $100,000 per key, for a total profit of over $2 million. We came out of it unscathed. We were on a roll once more. We'd gotten down to our last five keys in a month and a half.There was money everywhere. That's when Old Man Murphy and his law of "anything that can go wrong, will go wrong" came into play, and we had our first "accident."

We awoke early the next morning, and Marilyn drove my car, which contained the narcotics, back to L.A. I followed her on the freeway in one of my partner's trucks. I was enraged when she exited the freeway in El Segundo because she hadn't taken a direct route to the drop-off location. Aside from that, she'd exited in the worst conceivable spot, where three distinct sets of deputies patrolled on a regular basis. I gained her attention and convinced her to pull over. Don Vey and Baby Crim were directed to get that car back on the motorway. As fate would have it, a Los Angeles County sheriff's officer turned the corner just as they were pulling away from the curb. When we returned to the location of the chase, it was roped off with yellow crime-scene tape. My Lincoln was discovered with its doors, trunk, and hood wide open, clearly having been searched by deputies. I was worried not just about losing a couple hundred grand in narcotics, but also about the prospect that these guys might sing. To say the least, it was a hectic morning.

I'd never dealt with anything like this before. I went to Chinese Dave and Big Mike, whom I assumed would know how to operate it. Don and Crim were back on the streets in under an hour. Their bail was set at $50,000 each. It was the first time I met defense counsel Alan Fenster, a well-known narcotics lawyer in Los Angeles. He'd worked for Howard Wiseman, who had represented automaker John DeLorean in his infamous cocaine case. Alan had a large office in Beverly Hills, which amazed me. The criminal legal system was foreign to me, but Dave was well-versed in it. He went about Alan's office as if he owned it. Who'd have guessed? Perhaps he'd paid the office's rent multiple times over.

Alan Fenster agreed to represent Don Vey and Crim. I insisted that they do not waste any time. These guys were like brothers to me. They'd go to great lengths for me. And I wasn't about to send them to prison for narcotics possession that they weren't even earning from. I assured them that money was not an issue. I won't say how much I paid Fenster, but I will say it was the most I'd ever paid for anything other than narcotics. We would have been OK without the drug sale. But, after the arrest and confiscation of our Ready Rock, we were worse off than we were before we left for Miami. We had money on the street, but our drug supply was depleted. It was time to meet with Dave again.

Around that time, I had the opportunity to meet my drug hero, Thomas E. "Tootie" Reese. His name was known across town as the man who sold drugs. He'd just been arrested and made the top page of the Los Angeles Times, which was quite an accomplishment. I was cautious, but I wanted to meet him and talk to the man who the streets believed was the actual Super Fly. When we were out and about, people would point out his car, a red turbo Porsche. One of the construction workers suggested he could arrange a meeting between Tootie Reese and me. Inglewood is where I met him. It was a beautiful middle-class area in L.A.'s South Bay. The house appeared to be one of his storage locations. I also had my first encounter with Flint. We sat down to chat as a group.

Tootie informed me that he'd heard a lot about me and that my name was beginning to carry some weight. I swiftly decided against telling him that I idolized him growing up since I was beginning to suspect that I, too, was the man. The meeting also solidified my desire to be not only the biggest, but also the best drug dealer in Los Angeles, if not all of America. Nothing else would suffice. I believe it was something I'd picked up from tennis, this urge to be number one. When you have a goal that you can envision, feel, and nearly smell, you will do whatever it takes to get there.

It was time to return to Miami. Ollie and I were eager to see Dave. I mentioned the meeting when we arrived at Chinese Dave's residence. Dave exploded. I had no idea they were rivals. I had no idea they were dating the same woman. Tootie Reese may have thought Chinese Dave was attempting to whisk me away from him as well. I assured Dave that I was trustworthy. I kept telling myself that Tootie's pricing was already exorbitant. My primary concern at the time was returning to Miami to replenish. Ollie, Ton-ton, and I flew to Pensacola. The transaction went off without a hitch. We then drove up to Georgia to pick up an automobile. We'd begun looking in the newspaper for the automobile in advance, so it would be ready when we arrived. We discovered a 1975 Suburban. They demanded $2,000 for it, but we were able to negotiate a price of $1,500. Because my funds were so limited, the car was a financial hardship. After all was said and done, we only had around $3,500 left, which was very close. Fortunately, the Suburban was in good condition. It had lots of space, and we could make it if we took our time. We paid and drove away. Seating in a Suburban is divided into three rows. When I heard it, Ollie and Ton-ton had been sleeping in the back for a couple of hours.

The car was running out of gas. We had an issue. I went looking for the first exit. As the car came to a halt, we paid special heed to the road signs. I pulled off to the side of the road. The first thing we had to do was take the drug suitcase out of the car and hide it. That was handled by Ollie and Ton-ton, while I waved down cars in an attempt to secure us a ride. Finally, a man pulled over, broke his window, and assured us that he'd let a tow truck driver know where we were at the next exit. The gentleman kept his word. A tow truck driver arrived less than an hour later. We were overjoyed to meet him. The vehicle stopped over, got out, and inquired about the problem. I replied that I thought we had blown the engine. I inquired about the cost of towing us to a gas station. He worked in a police impound and junkyard and told us we could fix it there. For the tow, the cost would be $125. I was so cold at that moment that I didn't care where we were going or how much it would cost. The agreement was confirmed. While the Suburban was being connected up, Ollie sneaked back into the woods without the driver seeing and dropped the luggage back into the Suburban. We weren't concerned about going to a police impound yard.

We arrived at the yard and introduced ourselves to the owner. He was calm. I still believe he knew what we were up to. When he discovered we didn't have licenses, he offered to get us a rental car. That wasn't an option without a license. We didn't have any cash, but we did have a bag of cocaine worth millions. And there was no route back to California. Finally, we settled on a smaller U-Haul box truck, which the owner of the yard took us to pick up. There was barely enough room in the front seat for the three of us to transfer gears. Ollie stood around six feet two and had a strong physique with broad shoulders. Ton-ton stood probably around six feet tall and was stocky. As expected, I was assigned to the luxury seat in the middle.

Workers from the old neighborhood joined the team, but my brother David had a minor role in the drug trade. He wasn't very good at it, but he was very good at transporting the drugs and keeping the money and myself safe. He had that big brother attitude. I was still his baby brother to him. He kept an eye on me. The truck was equipped with a governor, which limited its top speed to 50 miles per hour. Our strategy was the same: take the long way around. We passed via Cincinnati, Kansas City, Denver, and ultimately arrived in Las Vegas. We were fortunate that the cops did not stop us. It was my first time staying in a hotel in Las Vegas. We had a good time. We had no cash on us, but we felt like millionaires. We were technically correct. We could get $200,000 a kilo at the time, so we had a bag of cocaine with us in Vegas with a street value of around $4 million. We went immediately back to work when we got home. Business began to pick up again. Things could not have gone any better. Friends, neighbors, and relatives in the neighborhood could see that we were doing well. They'd come after me for money. I kept about $40,000 in my pocket just for those times. Lorenzo "Zo" Murphy once informed me that his mother needed assistance. "She's dying," he explained. He burst into tears. "She needs surgery and doesn't have insurance." I spent $40,000 for her open-heart surgery, and his mother survived. Zo would never forget it.

According to Jim Galipeau, a probation officer in Los Angeles, I was "the biggest-time dope dealer to come up from the streets of South Central," and my reputation was enhanced by my avoidance of ostentatious jewelry, body tattoos, fancy cars, and designer clothes. One day, as I was leaving my mother's house after dropping off money, I noticed Henry, a Nicaraguan from my past, standing next to a car waiting for me. Henry worked as Ivan's assistant, or so it looked to us at the time. He was eventually revealed to be Danilo

Blandón's brother-in-law and a business partner of Ivan, our missing Nicaraguan supplier. "Hey, Ricky-man," Henry said, calling me over to his car in his half-broken English, "I need to talk to you." He wrapped his arm about me and inquired as to where I'd been. I glanced at him, perplexed, because he was the one who'd vanished for several months while we worked around the clock to recoup what we'd lost from their contact, Tony, in the snatch-and-grab poor coke deal. He informed me that Ivan wanted to speak with me. I could hear the frailty in Ivan's voice over the phone. Ivan was a huge man, six-foot-three and around 230 pounds, stocky and confident. But he sounded like a different person today, someone in horrible trouble. He invited me to pay him a visit. I assured him I'd be there whenever he needed me.

Ivan was in a motorized wheelchair at the hospital. He was half paralyzed and struggled to move the remote control for the chair. I could feel his anguish. He said he didn't want to converse in his room and requested us to accompany him outside. Once outdoors, Henry waited nearby, holding Ivan's drink, while Ivan sipped soda through a straw every now and then. He told us that he couldn't work because of his illness, and that Henry would take over. He stated that it would be business as usual. We informed him that we were no longer purchasing pounds, but only keys. We also claimed to have gotten them for $2,000 less than we had. We didn't inform him we were heading to Miami to pick them up. The meeting went well for Ollie and myself. We were delighted to meet Ivan, whom we considered a friend. We felt horrible for the guy, what with being shot in the back by his wife, but we were glad we had a source closer than Miami. We were curious if he could match the prices we were obtaining from Dave. We didn't have to worry because we had enough of cocaine. We simply want to establish more. When I awoke the next morning, there was a large yellow van parked in front of my house. A white-haired man was in the driver's seat. It was Ivan's driver,

Poppy. When I got outside, Poppy said, "Get in." Ivan, Henry, and another guy I'd never met were inside the van.

I took the money, which was hardly more than pocket change, and handed it over to them. If this was actually wonderful material, our company was about to explode. Poppy delivered the box that night. Ollie, JJ, Zo, and I went to the location and conducted a cook test. It passed, but it left yellowish rocks behind. We brought it to some smokers to put it through its paces. They adored it and renamed it. It was dubbed "Piss Yellow." I could see my future drastically better.

I phoned Chinese Dave and Big Mike and informed them of our lower price. We finally felt like we were on top of Dave. He was intrigued as to where I was obtaining it. I informed him that it was an old relationship. Ollie had previously dubbed Ivan "Ironside," after a TV lawyer played by Raymond Burr (better known as Perry Mason) who sat in his wheelchair yelling commands at people. We scheduled a time for Dave to see the product. I didn't tell him it was shaking so he wouldn't think it wasn't good quality. I didn't want to lose Dave as a customer. The first thing Dave did at his house was give it the old nose test. He snorted, then snorkeled, which caused his face muscles to spasm slightly. His expression told me he'd passed with flying colors. Then he had Nevel prepare some.

I knew it was all going to come back to haunt me. If you put a particular quantity in and cook it, you can observe what comes back out; this tells you how much cut was in the powder. There was no cut in this powder. It was the most pure I'd ever seen. It couldn't have been more natural than being on the farm in Nicaragua. We bargained about the price. I always attempted to have a relaxed demeanor. I wanted them to believe they were in charge of the entertainment. Dave, in particular, relished the opportunity. Of course, I knew the real figures and had already done some math.

Even though I'd just eliminated all the worry and difficulty of previous excursions, I'd added a hefty premium to the Miami ticket. I knew Dave wouldn't have anyone to accompany him to Florida if I didn't go. Besides, with this new hook-up, he'd have his drug when he released the money. Sometimes at the same hour. As the discussion came to a close, Dave, being the astute businessman that he was, agreed to all of my demands. That made me happy. With two guys I admired now working for me, it appeared that my time had come. Tootie Reese was sentenced to 35 years in jail. If necessary, I could control the flow of cocaine into the larger Los Angeles area. I was finally the man. As I heard about Tootie's lengthy term, it occurred to me that I could end myself in prison as well. But not in the same way as Tootie. So 1983 came to a close on a high note. I was making so much money that it didn't even matter. It ended up being where I did it for the rush.

The following year was out of this world. We moved between 50 and 100 keys per week. It was early 1984, I was 24, and I was a kingpin with more than a dozen crack homes in South Central making $20,000 to $40,000 per day. My drug dealer network was able to trade 500,000 crack rocks every day. By the end of 1984, I'd moved 100 keys per day. The news had traveled so far even my twin cousins in Texas had heard about it. They lived 1,800 miles away and were doing OK on their own. They traveled to California to inspect my setup. They were wearing enormous cowboy hats and ostrich-skin boots when I picked them up at the airport. It just so happened that the day I picked them up, I had a strong desire to experience the sensations of a Mercedes. I asked Maildog, one of my young men, if I could borrow his Benz, which was already set up. My cousins mistook the automobile for mine. I had homies take them over to a place and show them how to work a triple beam and cook it up—a crash course in the drug game. I suggested they visit the rest of the family when they finished the process. I also informed them that when they were ready to return to Texas, I'd have a package waiting for them and that they didn't have to pay for it.

When the time came, I packed them with eight ounces each, taped them to their sides, and loaded them onto the plane. I told them to yell at me when they returned to Texas, and they did. I received a phone call from Henry around this time. He was speaking quickly, and I could tell he was inebriated. When Henry walked up the driveway, I was leaning beneath the hood. As I went inside Henry's automobile, someone was sitting in the front passenger seat. I'd seen him before, but he'd never done anything more than nod or wave from afar. He did, however, extend his hand to me this time. "Good day, Ricky." "My name is Danilo." It was Danilo Blandón, a drug seller of practically pure coke straight from Nicaragua's cocaine farms.

# CHAPTER 15
# LORD OF THE DRUGS

I'd made an official connection with Danilo Blandón, which, unbeknownst to me at the time, would affect the trajectory of my life. Danilo, a stocky man with salt-and-pepper hair and a tidy mustache who conducted himself like a seasoned businessman, charged me $60,000 to meet. Danilo also spent 60 G's to meet me. With payments from each of us, Henry and Ivan were out of the picture, leaving Danilo and I to handle on our own. Ivan, on the other hand, was unaware of the introduction charge when it was reduced, and I was unaware that Ivan was unaware of it. Henry made a backhanded maneuver to acquire some quick cash. For me, it was direct access to cocaine from the source: Danilo. Danilo and I rolled around at our first meeting. We went to Rialto for dinner to talk about future business. Credit line offers were novel to me. I didn't think I needed it because my cash was stacking up. I was well over a million dollars and producing so much money that it was difficult for me to get to it. It's difficult to put into words. We couldn't keep up since the money was coming in so quickly and had to be tallied so frequently.

My first transaction with Danilo was for roughly 50 keys and took place barely a few hours after our initial meeting. It was the biggest and easiest drug deal the Freeway Boys and I had ever done. Danilo stowed the cocaine in the trunk of his brown silverfish Honda Civic, a lovely small four-door model. The car appeared to be spanking new. We never mixed drugs with money. Every sale after that went down the same way—clean, effortless, and far superior to the ones done in Miami, with Dave, and with Ivan. There was never any trust with Ivan until we hired Danilo. Ivan then altered his tune. As I already stated, I had no knowledge Henry had withdrawn Ivan from the arrangement. Not that I wouldn't have chosen Danilo regardless, but I didn't have a voice in the matter. As far as I knew, everything was legal.

Ivan's son let Ollie and me in and escorted us to Ivan's bedside, which was in a mechanically operated hospital bed. I felt sorry for him. Here was my friend, a man who had assisted me in becoming wealthy, and he was never going to walk again. He'd lost weight and appeared ill. Despite his illness, he wanted to conduct business. He laid everything out on the table. He thought Henry had crossed him, and he assumed I had as well. Before our meeting concluded, he mentioned that he was going to develop some new contacts in order to acquire competitive prices again, which would be fantastic for us. I'd benefit if they started competing for our business. His biggest concern was if I was still willing to collaborate with him. To show him that I was serious, I offered him a $10,000 gift and told him that he could ask for everything he needed. Before we departed, he stated that he would return to the game competitively, as he had previously. I trusted him. After that, Ollie and I talked about how everything was going and how, if everything went as planned, the money would start coming in. We didn't sell anything smaller than ounces. We had been completely evacuated from the streets. But things were about to change. Everything went as anticipated, and the money came in. I felt as though I were in a dream world. Because I was working constantly, my friends surprised me with a trip for my birthday.

They'd try to find something fresh to do because they said I only worked. I didn't think of what I was doing as a job or work. It was my big chance to make a name for myself and construct a future, and I relished it. For once, I'd discovered something that I thought I might excel at. Everyone aspires to be number one in tennis. In any sport, for that matter. I applied the same mindset to the drug trade, and I didn't want anyone or anything to stand in my way of reaching the top.

We arrived in Denver just before dusk, hopped off the plane, and boarded a commuter plane for the 45-minute ride to Aspen. From above, the snow-covered mountains looked stunning. We'd driven through Colorado before on one of our Miami visits, but it looked different this time; we weren't worried about being caught with 50 keys in the trunk. I was still smoking a lot of pot at the time. I'd gradually developed the habit. I could blame it on Ollie's constant smoking, but it simply kind of grew on me. The celebration contained cannabis. Our habit costs us approximately $30,000 every week. When I smoked, everyone else smoked, and it built up. My homies, on the other hand, had huge plans for the next day. One of them was on a snowmobile, which seemed like a fantastic idea at the moment. We'd all ridden dirt bikes, three-wheelers, and quads before, but none of us had ever ridden a snowmobile. We had no idea they didn't have brakes. We were around 40 people in all, and we hired all of the snowmobiles from the rental company. We began racing, then circled the track to see who could go the fastest. Following that, we played bumper mobile. Some of the girls had already wiped out, drove over fences, or wiped out. It was complete anarchy.

This lasted nearly four hours. After we finished, we went around collecting all of the broken snowmobiles and fences. The proprietor was furious. Several snowmobiles had to be dragged back. I informed the owner that we would cover all repair and replacement expenses. Everyone on the trip was either ghetto affluent or a member of my personal crew, so money was never an issue. I spent roughly $40,000 on the four hours on the snowmobiles. I called Mary, and she sent an overnight cashier's check. Mary was in charge of all financial matters. I knew I could always rely on her. Her house, on 88th Street between Grand and Broadway, was our first money-counting location. She was also far more organized than the rest of us. Mary had everyone's phone numbers and knew who was short on cash and who was not. Mary was like a mother to me, and Karen, her daughter, was like a sister to me. I handed the check to the proprietor and assured him we'd be back in the morning. The next day, he stated he wouldn't let us back on his snowmobiles. I realized what you meant. Everything was going well and everyone was having a nice time until Ingrid, also known as Goldie, who worked for me, tried to catch her balance instead of learning how to stop on skis and crashed into a building. Fortunately, she was not wounded, but that was the end of Goldie's skiing career. Because she was fine—just shaken up—the rest of us went skiing and had a nice time. During that trip, I fell in love with skiing.

Back in the city, business was thriving. It was approximately 1985 that I coined the phrase "doubling-up." It wasn't really my idea; I happened upon it. Marilyn, my Main Street sweetheart, had a team of females working for her, and I'd give her approximately eight ounces a day to keep her out of my hair. The essential point here was that she'd made it such that anyone with a hundred dollars could get a rock. Anyone could afford it with that notion. The key to a good product is making it affordable to everyone, not just the privileged few, and Marilyn had worked that out, owing to her tiny quantity and passing on the price reduction to her clients. Without understanding it at first, it was an economic model that we were testing. This was a good concept. I dashed out to get the guys, and we returned to Marilyn's at 97th and Hoover. One thing I enjoyed was that the consumers didn't complain, dispute about prices, or try to bargain. They waited in line, bought their weed, and then left. It was straightforward. Many of the folks I assisted get started had risen to prominence by this point. They had several hundred thousand bucks and would fight over price. It gave me a headache. But this way, I'd be able to put the squeeze on them.

I had a strategy. This was intended to be our first "mega-rock house," as I dubbed it. Ollie, Renzo, Tootie, Little Steve, and I all invested in the venture together. When we arrived, the guys noticed a line extending from the side of the house as we approached. It made an impression on me. Marilyn was disliked by all of the homies. She frequently flaunted her power, letting everyone know she was Ricky's girl. Some of the guys misinterpreted it. I could see them taking it in and understanding the potential once we got inside and I explained the process to them. I assured them that by doing it this way, we'd be making $1,400 per ounce instead of a thousand or even less. It was straightforward reasoning.

I got Joe, JJ, and Tootie to take over the house. Marilyn was initially irritated because she believed she was being excluded. My word was final at the end of the day. I assured her I'd tell her what I had in mind for her that night. My thoughts were racing. That mansion alone might bring in up to $40,000 every day, yet the rent was only $450 per month, which was reasonable. Many of the homies still couldn't stand on their own two feet. The house and its possibilities would make things easier for them. We weren't concerned about the cops because the individuals in line outside weren't junkies; they were middle-class people with a crack problem. My brother David used to claim that the crack lines were often 60 people thick, "like waiting for a Magic Mountain thrill ride at Disneyland," only they were waiting for the excitement of the crack.

When Marilyn and I got home that night, I told her I was putting her in charge of finding the houses. She'd evolved into my main lady. She'd still have all the money she needed, but she wouldn't be sitting in a rock house. I'd keep letting her cook and cut the dope, which Marilyn and her crew took time and delight in doing so that each rock was smooth and even. They were excellent at it. Things were looking well for Marilyn and her team. I went by all the tracks and told everyone I knew—smokers and hustlers alike—that I'd just opened a site nearby, gave them the address, and used the term "double-up." That meant that if they paid $100 for a two-gram rock, they could keep one gram and sell the other for the same amount. It was a hit with the smoking hustlers.

Most of the time, they got it because they were the foundation of my business, and I couldn't abandon them. At the same time, I was aware that the majority of my homeboys were still missing the broader picture. As a test, I'd give the guys a half-ounce or even an ounce on a few occasions. When money was ample, I'd do it around the first of the month. I was curious about how long the drugs and money would last. It didn't take long for them to run out of both. They may begin the month with $4,000 and be finished in 10 days. I repeated the experiment with $100 rocks for those that smoked. The issue was that they couldn't get up from the table once they started. The issue about cocaine is that it makes folks feel like they've had more than they have.

The houses scattered all over the place. We had perhaps seven or eight of them, each with what I dubbed McDonald's small drive-through windows for quick, efficient service. They'd be busy as soon as we opened the doors. I designed a structure for the dwellings. The heads of the houses would be all of the principal men who had been working with me since the beginning. It would be their responsibility to go to the 'hood and recruit three kids to work in the houses. We also held a competition to see which house would generate the greatest revenue. Each head of the house earned $5,000 per week, and his employees earned $400 each. There was no cost for food or cannabis. Another person, Paul, was in charge of handing off work or narcotics and picking up money.

Something strange happened during this time. We were at 79th and Avalon, where there was a quarter-pound house. I was speaking with one of the young staffers, "Dollar." Dollar had been falling short with no explanation. Needless to say, the problem resolved itself, and Dollar became one of our top dealers. He worked with me until he and my cousin Tootie were jailed in Dallas at the end of 1986. Then, one after the other, mishaps occurred. I received a phone call about six a.m. one morning. I was told that my cousin Eric had just slain his fiancée, Joy, at one of our favorite hangouts. I stood up and began investigating right away. I had to be kind with a couple of my team members, the most important of whom was Eric. These were hot heads who were fast to grab a pistol. And I knew that if I pushed them at the wrong time, they'd pull down on me.

That house has to be closed down. The cops swamped the neighborhood, questioning everyone. I'm sure Joy's people told them who we were and what we were up to. This was not the catalyst for the formation of the "Freeway Ricky Task Force," but it surely didn't help matters. And situations like these continued happening. The second occurrence occurred when I went to 81st Street in search of Big June Bug. He'd taken over 81st, my original position. He and Juda Bean were putting together the Hoover Crips. The gangbangers were now known as The Hoover Connect. June Bug was one of the strangest little motherfuckers I'd ever met. And word had spread that he was out for vengeance. Things were flying off the hook. As if the heat wasn't enough, three people were slain in the same region a few weeks later. The three were said to be the ones responsible for the attack on Big June Bug. There were cops and narcos everywhere. I was expecting my name to be called.

But you can't hide when you hire the best personalities in the industry. They made their names through gangbanging. They were drug dealers for me, and everything they did on their own had nothing to do with me. However, because I was affiliated with them, the officers quickly linked me to the violent gangbanging they engaged in. In retrospect, situations like this are what stoked the fire for law enforcement to form the Freeway Ricky Task Force with the sole purpose of putting me out of business and sending me down. Another issue was that I was slipping in and out of the neighborhood.

I wasn't hanging out on the sidewalk. Overall, 1984 was shaping up to be a terrific year, with plenty of business, contacts, and women. The Freeway Boys were having a terrific time. The cops, on the other hand, were still sniffing around, making it difficult to relax. We'd gotten to the point where we were moving anywhere from 125 to 150 keys per day and buying 40 to 50 kilos at a time from Danilo Blandón. The essential pricing had dropped into the teens, making it much more affordable for us, and we passed the savings on to our clients. Everything seemed to be going swimmingly.

Money poured in by the bag load. The only problem was that I was getting bored. I wanted to diversify my business. So I created the Big Palace of Wheels tire and auto parts store on Western Avenue and enjoyed assisting people. I scrubbed cars and flirted with women on hot days. It had been one of those days. Chris Young, one of my primary men, arrived. Chris has a habit of hanging out with money. He enjoyed dealing with the bigwigs. We hit a $75,000 lick from one of his guys in Seattle the first night we even got together. Every time we got together, he seemed to have a 10- or 15-sale lined up. I had a penchant for making others feel special. And I had no issue demonstrating to Chris how unique he was in my eyes.

The feds had raided Den's residence, along with four others, not long earlier. They discovered a large amount of narcotics, money, and machine weapons at Den's house. He was the absolute last person I wanted to talk to. I disliked talking to folks who were incarcerated. Especially when it comes to drugs. But this was Chris, and Den was cool, so I answered the phone. Den had always been a clown. He started off by laughing and playing. He didn't sound like a prisoner to me. But then he said he was at Terminal Island and that my name was being called. People are saying things like, "Things must be flowing on the Freeway." He warned me to be cautious. I took his admonition to heart.

As I handed the phone back to Chris, I had visions of going to prison. Den's business had been handled by Kenny Ray while he was away. I'd just seen him a few days prior, right before he went to jail. I owned the repair shop, as well as a 22-unit motel named the Freeway Motor Inn and a junkyard that also sold used cars. The aura surrounding those firms was not the same as it was around the drug trade. I began to consider new frontiers. If this place didn't require me anymore and I could get my money without any effort, the goal became acquiring new regions. I'd been attempting to persuade the guys to delve into uncharted territory for quite some time. But they felt more at ease being under my wing. So, once again, if any ground were to be broken, I'd have to be the one to break it. It surprised me that my guys had all of the necessary abilities to go out on their own but were hesitant to do so.

I'd decided that once I finished the hotel, I'd relocate to St. Louis, Missouri. I'd never been there, but I had a guy from high school, Tony Wingo, who was from St. Louis. To me, he was like a big brother. We didn't communicate much. When he returned, I wasn't the same Little Ricky he'd known. I didn't want lawn service anymore, but he did. And, because he was like family, he started a lawn service the same day he asked about starting a business with him. He also received the contract for my houses, so he was in business right away. Tony and I were tense once more. We'd regularly run into each other at the houses when I checked up on the guys and Tony was working on the grounds. I met him again at one of the residences, and he mentioned that he had a brother in St. Louis who was selling marijuana and would like to get in on the action. I told him I was eager to meet his brother and asked him to let me know when he could travel out to see me. I offered to pay for his plane ticket. Soon after, Mike Wingo, the brother, arrived in Los Angeles, and we had our first sit-down encounter.

I'd learned a lot about how to get folks started in the drug business. I'd learnt via trial and error and was familiar with some of the traps and pitfalls on both sides. But I'd gotten the hang of it by this point. When we sat down to discuss, I told him about my drug use. I had no idea what a gram was worth in St. Louis at the time, but I made an educated guess. They were worth between $150 and $200 per gram. I intended to give him two ounces as a starter package for free. I'd do that so he could perform some market research for me. We reached an agreement, and he left for St. Louis.

Then Tony's younger sister and boyfriend wanted to join in. They took off on their own. Kim, his sister, became close to Marilyn. I felt it'd be a wonderful opportunity for them to get into the game because they were similar in age. Around the same time, Maicha's father, Indian Tommy, who lived in Cincinnati, approached us with his hand out. He used to smoke when he lived in California. He and his girlfriend, Smoke, had relocated to Cincinnati to begin a new life. Smoke had always impressed me since she took care of her own affairs. The amount of medications I gave them to get started had no negative impact on the business. It resulted in the creation of more businesses, but solely outside of town. Other than Texas and Florida, I had not traveled outside of California. But a voice in my head kept telling me I should go to St. Louis and Cincinnati. With Indian Tommy and Smoke purchasing two keys each month, Mike in St. Louis purchasing two keys, and Billy purchasing approximately three keys every month, business was brisk. The money was sufficient to finance a trip to see the business. I didn't realize it at the time, but the Midwest locations were the start of the end. And I wasn't expecting it.

# CHAPTER 16
# DIRTY COPS

I found a great downtown St. Louis condominium to rent. I was waiting for the manager to complete the papers and get the unit ready for the move-in. Instead of staying alone in a motel room, I spent most evenings at Mike Wingo's residence. Everything was going swimmingly. JJ then called with horrible news. Ollie was doing my old job at this point: checking on houses, picking up cash, riding horses, and flying model planes. The vital stuff, you know. JJ was in charge of the day-to-day activities. He was the conduit for everything.

"The cops raided Marilyn's house," JJ reported.
Marilyn, her brother Steve, and my brother Tootie were all arrested. It was perplexing because Marilyn, like the rest of us, had never kept narcotics in our homes. We kept the cocaine in various stash cars parked a few homes away. JJ told me that day that 50 birds, or kilograms, were in the car on the street near the busted house. It was a good load that we didn't want to lose. Nobody wants to get caught with 50 keys. JJ assured me that the car was secure. He assured me that the automobile had been transferred carefully. I didn't want any of my employees to be locked up. I requested JJ to contact attorney Alan Fenster about the cases, get everyone out of jail as soon as possible, and keep me updated on any developments. I also informed him that everything was going fine in St. Louis. I wanted the guys to come to St. Louis after I got my place set up. I got another page about three hours after the first one. Marilyn was released after JJ posted her bail.

I hopped on the next flight out, and JJ and Ollie met me at LAX. They filled me in on the way from the airport. Stevie had been visiting Marilyn and our infant daughter, Rikiya. While the cops were still present, my cousin Tootie and his wife went to Marilyn's to pick up our kid. The cops kicked Steven and Tootie in the shins. The officers also forced them to put on my clothes from home to see if they fit and to determine which of them was Freeway Rick Ross. There were no images of me at Marilyn's house, so the cops had no idea who I was. I'd been in Los Angeles for three days when Tony arrived at my body shop on 65th and San Pedro, in the large yellow Dually vehicle I'd given him. I knew something was awry when I saw him approaching. He delivered more awful news to me. Mike was detained in St. Louis.

Mike was apprehended not only with what he had, but also with four kilos I'd placed in the trunk of my car. I promised Mike's father the automobile a few days before I went because I didn't need it anymore. I spent only $4,500 for it, and it had a clear title. I'd have $400,000 after selling those four keys. I figured the least I could do was give his father, who was one of my assistants, a car. But Mike had acted too quickly. He'd removed the four keys from the automobile and delivered them to his father. He took a block from his basement wall and hid the cocaine behind it. It only got worse. Mike was selling narcotics from his home, where his family was staying. In my circles, this was unheard of. It was just not our style. Mike had made a critical error. I then realized I'd been flying under my true identity. There was a considerable chance I'd left the plane ticket stubs at Mike's place, which could be used to charge me with drug trafficking.

I was wondering what was going on from 2,000 miles away. I'd been called away from St. Louis because of problems in L.A., and now I'm in L.A., hearing about problems in St. Louis. I was also concerned about Mike and his family. I wanted to protect Mike's family, so I had his wife post the bond and found the best lawyer in town. I was still making a killing in L.A., so a $200,000 or $300,000 loss on bail in St. Louis wouldn't put me out of business. Marilyn, Tootie, and

Stevie's bail was set at $50,000 each, but I only had to pay 10% bond and put up collateral, so it wasn't too bad.

My attorney, on the other hand, Alan Fenster, had gotten to the point where every case he handled cost me $50,000 or more. My plan was that if I kept all of them out of jail, I would stay out as well. So I gave Alan a sizable retainer. It was around this period that my lawyer and I discussed corrupt officers. Around the same time, my brother David had an odd run-in with the cops, which confirmed that we were dealing with crooked officers, guys who would do virtually anything to obtain their man, dope, and cash. "We're being followed," the driver said a few minutes after David and some homeboys departed the Big Palace of Wheels. They eventually lost the tail and came to a stop on Ventura Boulevard at a petrol station. The gas station employee pointed across the street to a parked Los Angeles County Sheriff's Department black-and-white car and said, "That's the fuckheads."However, the black-and-white pursued them to the interstate and pulled them over. Then they heard the cop proclaim over the radio that he had them. Just thereafter, a California Highway Patrol trooper drove over behind them.

He was correct. Police and sheriff's deputies patrolled city and county highways and streets, while the Highway Patrol patrolled freeways and interstates. The deputy let them go, but followed them all the way to Sylmar, California, where they exited the freeway. He pulled over their automobile and waited for drug cops. When the narcs arrived, they dragged David and his buddies out of the car and ordered them to spread their legs and place their hands on the car roof. What transpired next confirmed that we were dealing with corrupt cops. A deputy searched the car without probable cause or a warrant and emerged with a bag of dope, despite the fact that David and the homies had no cocaine on them. The strange thing was that the deputies did not arrest them. Then one of the narcos shot David in the back of the skull with a gun butt. Following the departure of the cops, the homies summoned an ambulance, which transported him to Valencia Hospital. For a while, he had a massive knot on his head.

People still wanted all the dope I could get my hands on, so I obtained 100 keys. I decided to make coke one night. But before I began, I received an unexpected phone call from Danilo, ordering me to wait. The cocaine keys were safely in the trunk of a car in the parking area of our Brentwood apartment complex. I hadn't been to the Comedy Club in a while, so I figured, why not? After all, I'm not going to cook tonight. I'll have a good time with my buddies. I instructed the tiny homies to remain low, take the bucket, and have a good time since I was heading to the Comedy Club and will page them first thing in the morning. We then went to the club. The place was full, but Ollie had arranged for us to skip the line with the doorman. We walked right through. We had a great time coming to the Comedy Club and teasing the comedians. We'd frequently make the show more lively. Comedians who went on to become renowned were just getting started there, trying their hand at stand-up. Even though Robin Harris did a fantastic job, it was difficult to follow Rodney Dangerfield. When he called us Sherm Heads, the entire building went berserk. He and I were on the same wavelength. The night was going swimmingly.

As we drove away, I turned into Sunset Boulevard. At 2 a.m., the Strip was still alive with activity. On the Strip, we noticed the occasional prostitute. They were a more sophisticated group, and Ollie enjoyed playing with them, rolling down the window and talking to them as we drove. We arrived at Ollie and Robert's apartment at 2:30 p.m., and I dropped them off. Ollie had arranged for us to meet at the Bonaventure Hotel. She dialed the number and gave me the room number. Once the cops were on my tail, I lived that way. That night, in the room, a bath was already prepared and waiting for me. Marilyn, my girl, understood how to look after me.

My pager beeps as soon as I come out and starts drying off. Alan Fenster's phone number. What the hell could he possibly want at three a.m.? I dialed his number. He informed me that the police had apprehended Ollie and Robert. The cops were on us again, exactly as Danilo had predicted.

I promised him I'd take care of whatever it cost, knowing full well that it would be exorbitant. Then I called Jocelyn, another homegirl who helped out, and urged her to contact the bondsman and have them released as soon as possible. I got Ollie and Robert out of jail, but a few days later, two DEA officers, one from Los Angeles and the other from St. Louis, showed up to my mother's house, one from Los Angeles and the other from St. Louis, to personally present me an indictment from St. Louis. Because I was not present, they left their business cards and the indictment. My mother called to tell me that St. Louis wanted to speak with me about the four keys they discovered inside Mike's residence. She went to Alan Fenster's law office with the indictment. Alan called to inform me that there was now an outstanding arrest warrant for me. He inquired as to what I intended to do. I didn't want to go to jail right now, so I asked if he could look into getting me bail. Alan told the two DEA agents that the LAPD and the Los Angeles County Sheriff's Department had been following me for two years and hadn't found anything tangible against me. He told them that if they awarded me $50,000 bail, I'd appear in federal court in two weeks. They both agreed. I was living on pins and needles. I didn't want to go to jail, especially for an extended amount of time. I didn't plan on staying long, but the prospect gave me the shivers. I stayed busy at work.

Danilo kept urging me to buy, and we saw him almost every day. When Danilo came by one of our residences, we sat back and Ollie showed off his new 22-caliber pistol. Danilo showed up the next day with an Uzi submachine gun still in its original packaging and gave it to Ollie. Then he handed me a.22 rifle with a silencer. If Danilo was trying to impress us, he was succeeding. I was so confident that I wouldn't go to jail that I arranged to pick up 50 keys from Danilo on the same day I was supposed to turn myself in to the police. I expected a fast trip to the federal courthouse and a quick release on bail. On the appointed surrender day, I appeared in court with Marilyn, my mother, and Alan Fenster. We were also accompanied by the bail bondsman, who had the $50,000 bail money in hand as part of our deal with the DEA. The judge authorized the deal at the end of the session. Sitting on those iron seats in that jail wore on my spirit. It felt chilly, uncomfortably warm, and stale. I'm sure the conditions influence defendants' mental states, leading them to accept plea bargains rather than languish in jail awaiting their trials. As I strolled down the corridor, they informed me that my girlfriend was waiting for me in the lobby. It was a great sight to see Marilyn. As it turned out, Mike Wingo refused to testify against me, thus the case was dismissed for lack of evidence. I was free to go.

I went into work mode as soon as I was discharged. I had some business to attend to. Marilyn drove a few blocks before stopping at a phone booth to let me contact Danilo. Danilo handed me the keys to a brown Honda stopped on the side of the road for the car switch. I followed Danilo out to the parking lot, near where Marilyn was waiting in her car, and instructed her to keep her distance. We picked up the cash, and Danilo drove his Honda back to his house. The transaction went smoothly. The gang had turned into quite the party animals. And my Texas cousins had no trouble getting in, smashing up clubs with them. The homies seemed to riot in the Hobart Club every night of the week lately. The proprietors would often shake me down for money to pay for anything the guys had ripped up the night before. I invited the guys to meet me at Twin Sisters, one of our favorite brunch spots. It probably hardly held 20 people, but the meal was delicious and we were properly taken care of. Also, one of the owner's daughters was excellent, providing us with just enough action to keep us coming back for more. To my knowledge, none of the homies ever hit on her, which was unusual, but they did enjoy her company at the restaurant. So that place was cool for a variety of reasons.

I told the gang I'd brought up 50 chickens (our slang for kilos). They were astonished because they expected me to tone down the buying and selling because there was so much heat surrounding me and I'd been out doing my own thing, letting them manage the day-to-day business. I could see they were relieved I was still alive and had gotten released on bond. When I mentioned that I was returning and would be involved in the day-to-day activities again, everyone smiled. Robert and Ollie, on the other hand, couldn't dodge the cops since they headed home. Ollie returned home, shut the front door, and was on his way to his bedroom when he heard an explosion in the front yard. He instinctively reached for his revolver, which was hidden beneath a cushion on his bed. Then he recognized it wasn't the work of a burglar, thief, or gang member. The cops used it as a battering hammer against his home door. He retracted his rifle and waited. The cavalry stormed into his chamber and shackled his hands behind his back. He expected them to search for drugs first, but not these cops. They wanted cold, hard cash, and when they unlocked Ollie's closet and saw the two-ton safe resting on the floor, they felt they'd struck gold. Ollie's safe served as a temporary cash stash.

Unfortunately for them, I'd already emptied the safe and transported it to a stash house. Ollie didn't tell them it was empty; he let them investigate for themselves. The cops were not thrilled to discover it empty, so they forced Ollie, Robert's roommate, onto the floor next to his safe, then placed $40,000 inside the safe, along with half a crack key, and took photos for evidence. It was a down-and-dirty set-up. We never mixed crack and money; that wasn't our style. But the cops were unaware of this. To be honest, I had no idea how I was going to bail Ollie and Robert out of this situation. They were both really apprehensive about it. It didn't seem promising for either of them.

We reacted and adjusted to the new circumstances as usual. We began creating one or two drops every day because we were now only selling in large quantities. We counted money the remainder of the time. We were making a few hundred thousand dollars per day by selling 10 to 15 keys. We made plans to relocate from Los Angeles to Westwood. It was near the campus of the University of California, Los Angeles, where backpacks were ubiquitous. We had Steve, June, and Nigh deliver the narcotics on bicycles, and we planned four meeting points for the homies. The only big issue was locating cookhouses. Cooking was when we were most vulnerable since it took so much time. It took about four to six hours to fry 100 keys. So, after putting everything back on track, my mission was to find safer ways to cook. I'd heard of folks I'd sold cocaine to reselling it as "cocaine hard," or "ready made," which was cheaper than the powder I was selling. The word on the street was that the quality was excellent—even exceptional. I soon discovered it was known as "blow-up." Naturally, I was interested in how they did it.

Watts was buzzing with tales of a blow-up. Watts was run by my boy Chubbs. I went to Jordan Downs, a Watts housing project bounded on the west by Grape Street, the north by 97th Street, the east by Alameda Street, and the south by 103rd Street. It was rockin' and rollin' when I got into the parking lot. When I got out of my automobile, everyone looked at me. It was a tense situation. I'm not sure how they knew I didn't belong, but they did. It appeared to be similar to some of our drug-selling music, but a few notches worse. When I asked to speak with Chubbs, they relaxed a little. Initially, I assumed Chubbs was merely a gangbanger who'd made some money because he knew Honcho and later met me. He wasn't sure how many keys I was buying at a time, but he had an idea. He'd also introduced me to some great names, such as Dennis Tortin and

Cookie. We discussed the blow-up game. The smile on his face told me he knew I was asking about producing crack. He accompanied me back to my car.

That evening, Chubbs and I met at my flat on 79th and Avalon. I barricaded the place like Fort Knox. When police eventually raided it, it took them an hour and a half to get inside. The officers informed my guys that once they got inside, they were going to beat some ass, and they did. JJ and Zo brought over the key, and my top people were present to observe how it was done firsthand. The fellas had slipped since I'd been gone. There was a lot going on in the neighborhood that I wasn't aware of, including a new technique to cook. I should have known better. I wanted to fine-tune everything now. He'd taken two of his assistants with him. They shattered the first key and fried it up. I saw what they put in there, but I had no idea what it was. They finished with 16 ounces more than he started with. And it still looked as good as it did when it was raw. I wasn't completely convinced. A smoke test was required. JJ and Zo were dispatched to find us a cigarette. This crack stuff stood up to scrutiny. It was incredible: an extra 16 ounces on each key. It was like getting a free pound. It felt like a ruse.

The only problem was that Chubbs refused to give up the recipe, which I couldn't blame him for. Chubbs told me after he cooked for us that if we wanted him to cook for us again, it would be $20,000 at a time. So Chubbs volunteered to be our cook. This lasted four days. JJ then radioed in to say he'd figured it out. I went over soon away, and sure enough, he had. This left me in a difficult position, because Chubbs was my kid, and I didn't want to beat him up. I called him and explained everything. We decided to meet for lunch at Fat Momma's. We left the restaurant and went to the quarter-pounder. They had about $35,000 on hand. I handed him that and promised him the remainder later that night. Following that, business was as smooth as a run on fresh powder on freshly waxed skis. All police action seemed to have stopped, and there was love in the 'hood for everyone. For the next nine months, business was at an all-time high, and it seemed like there was nothing we could do wrong. I was bored once more because everything was working nicely and my guys were taking care of business. I got into real estate by purchasing and repairing ancient houses. But I was missing something. I needed some action. My crew guys, Little Tommy and Black Tommy, raced one of the Browning Brothers from Pasadena. Black Tommy was recognized as the city's best drag racer, and man, could he ride a bike. He eventually rose to national prominence on the NORA circuit. He may have finished in the top three in the world. I had Black Tommy teach me to bike after seeing Little Tommy ride. When we initially met, Black Tommy was Little Tommy's cocaine customer, but as we spent more time together, that naturally changed. I didn't like interrupting individuals in the middle of their transactions, so Black Tommy devised a fantastic solution. He stated he'd continue to work for Little Tommy, but he wanted to buy some for himself. That didn't bother me in the least. I believed that everyone should take their money and invest it.

We went to a shop and bought two bikes with electronic shifters for $6,000 apiece. They were quick, so I could get a feel for it. Then came Black. Tommy advised me that if I truly wanted to go fast, I should acquire a Vance and Hines bike, so we went to their shop in Industry. While we were discussing, the company's president came in and told me about a bike he'd just made. Bryant had completed the work, but the specifications had been completed by the president. They anticipated that it would break the world record. They asked me to look at it next weekend at a race. We went to the races that weekend, and the bike, as they stated, broke the world record. Bryant sold the bike to me. I figured that with a fast bike, I could be the fastest in the pro comp category. I began constructing a pro-stock race car for myself. I was looking for excitement. Time would show that I was wasting my time on frivolous activities.

# CHAPTER 17
# RAIDS BY THE POLICE

As we drove down Main Street, we noticed a bustle as we got closer to the pool hall. We passed past slowly and without pausing. It appeared to be a police raid. We drove a few blocks to a parking lot where we could observe. We saw cops in green jackets coming in and out of the building. Ollie and I were worried about the homies inside, but not too worried; we knew there was no dope inside, because that's not how the guys functioned in order to protect themselves from this particular situation. We initially sat in the car and laughed. The cops left after about 30 minutes. We sat back and waited for them to leave before going in to check on everyone. An ambulance arrived as we neared the front door. When we arrived, the apartment was in wreckage, with several of the homies injured.

It appeared to be something out of a TV cop show. The guys were complaining about their limbs, and some of them had enormous knots on their heads. It was difficult to comprehend that cops had thrown pool tables on these men's backs while they were handcuffed and had struck them over the head with pool balls and clubs. The Cruz situation remained a mystery. We had a serious situation on our hands. Ollie and I didn't stay long. I sought to figure out who these cops who utilized those tactics were. I wondered if they conducted any preliminary investigation, because it appeared like they'd simply picked a location where we hung out and raided it, even if we weren't selling dope there.

I began wearing disguises in public places, such as Manchester Park, and anytime I went out to conduct business. The park had essentially become a ghost town. After a few people were slain, parents no longer wanted their children to go there. But we saw it as our park, so we seized control and turned it around. We had the ability, so we used it to make Manchester Park a safer place. It became a safe haven, a location where Bloods could freely wear red in the heart of a Crips 'hood without fear of reprisal. My days were spent going from gym to gym seeking for pick-up games. The park director, Mr. King, had given us keys to the Manchester Park gym, so we could play anytime we wanted. We were regularly bringing Mr. King lunch. I also bought fiberglass backboards with breakaway rims, for which he was grateful. The gym quickly became a popular meeting place. Everyone in the neighborhood started sponsoring teams. The gym was packed for the playoffs for the league I sponsored.

When I arrived at the gym one day, Tony T, an original customer, ran up to me. He showed me the kind of affection that you don't often see. He patrolled the park from end to end whenever he knew I was there. He and I got into the habit of communicating in code and riddles. He never addressed me as Rick. It was always "J.R." after the Dallas character J.R. Ross Ewing. Tony noticed police surrounding the area and issued a warning that the cops were about to raid the park. It was a warning to the homies to fasten their straps. We rushed into Mr. King's office, where the boys were putting their straps in his closet—and not a second too soon. The park was encircled by narcotics agents, plainclothes detectives, and black-and-white police units. People rushed past the police barricades to escape. Unnoticed, I jumped right in. My low-key demeanor had paid off, as it had gotten me out of the park and away from the raid without being noticed.

I walked down the street calmly, to my mother's house, and got her car. It made me laugh out loud. Those cops were perplexed.I'd heard urban legends that I'd created caverns beneath the streets, like if I possessed some kind of superpower. The fact was far more straightforward. Maybe it was simply my ego, but my confidence was building. I was determined to grow the company. I still desired to be the largest and best. The cops were equally determined to bring us to justice. They started trying new strategies, or at least new to us. They started assaulting our customers because they rarely discovered dope on us.

The cops discovered the narcotics and money. They also gave Cliff a nice whoopin', but they let him go. The cops couldn't blame him because the residence was not in his name. We always stayed in smokers' homes or apartments. They informed Cliff that they knew he was getting dope from me and warned him that I was going down hard. The cops then apprehended J.C. Chapman at 93rd and Normandie, where they discovered him with a tiny amount of cocaine. J.C. was also beaten up, but unlike Cliff, he was charged with possession. J.C.'s location was rockin' so hard that he reopened that night, after being freed on bond, without missing a beat. But he was back in jail within two days. After catching a case in Oklahoma, he was later convicted and sentenced to life in prison for two earlier offenses. Then there was "Stupid," who was actually Bret. He certainly lived up to his moniker. Bret was of Swaun descent. I recognized him from my days of low-riding. When the officers raided Bret's house, it was the first time I'd heard of many simultaneous raids. It was a new police tactic. The cops seized a large amount of marijuana from Bret, estimated to be nine keys of hard ounces. Ken, Bret's older brother, was a welder who enjoyed making things. Ken stated that the way we barred up our houses was incorrect. The officers' new battering ram made it easier for them to enter our homes if they hit us. But the manner Ken barricaded Bret's house introduced a whole new technique to barricade houses. It slowed the cops down so much that by the time they arrived, Bret had already flushed the drugs. He was sitting on his couch at the time, watching a video.

# CHAPTER 18
# COUNTING MONEY

My best years were 1985 and 1986. Things were almost too good to be true. I sold all the marijuana I could get my hands on at reasonable prices. I'd worked my way up the food chain and had four solid hookups by this point. Furthermore, I frequently bid them against each other. All of these guys used to be friends, and I played that up to get the pricing I wanted, despite being well aware of how easily money can come between friendships. Now that I had a count house in South Central, we knew everyone on the block. Nobody was going to tell us, especially since it was just a count house. There were never any drugs present. The only money dumped was $100,000 or more, and the majority of employees dropped their money and left. I spent the majority of my time there. Our major clients began to spend time there as well, chatting and negotiating costs.

With individuals pouring in and out and cops watching our every move, I implemented security measures. To synchronize our movements and keep our communications covert, we had the walkie-talkie system locked onto a private channel. I also had a crew close to me—in business, they'd be my administrative team in the executive branch—who were paid $1,000 a week to function as crack cookers, money counters, bodyguards, lookouts, and drivers. I had people who only did one thing: dispose of possibly damning material. Big Mike and Chinese Dave were by far my most important employees. And as a method of rewarding them for their efforts, I set a price to reflect that. Mary sat at her desk, counting money like she always did. As the bills rolled off the money machine, I heard it clap. I was gathering funds to purchase my first 100 keys, but first I had to persuade them to reduce the price from $37,000 to $35,000 or perhaps $34,000 per key. Every day, I required 100 to 200 keys to get through and keep my guys working. They were now selling my coke in almost every major city west of the Mississippi River.

A loud beating on the door jolted me out of my reverie. To scare me, the homies would pound on the doors as if they were cops. When I peeked out the window, I noticed JJ, Renzo, Tootie, and Kenny. They'd been collecting money and had brought in six Nike gym bags full of cash. I inquired about Big Mike. He was one of the big homies and was notorious for being stingy with his money. I needed money for the 100 deal to go through. I wasn't going to take any chances. I paid Mary well to count. That's exactly what she intended to accomplish. Seeing money being tallied made me hungry, so my homeboys and I went out for M&Ms. On the way back down Florence, Lil' Steve, who had joined us, pointed out a bunch of narc cars on the road. Even though we were clean, my radar went on high alert, my blood pressure soared, and my pulse pounded quicker by the second. When it comes to gambling, you can never be too safe.

Cop cars sped up as we reached Van Ness. Maybe they're spying on us, I reasoned. Then, at the last possible moment, they swerved around us and turned right onto Van Ness. They were clearly hitting someone in our area. Half of me wished I could follow them to see what was going on. The other half had a list of 100 keys in mind. When we returned to the counting house, we found a few of our clients, as well as Big Mike and Chinese Dave. It seemed to quiet down when we entered the room. Mary waved me over as she stacked money and wrapped cash in rubber bands with one hand. I knelt down and she whispered, "Chinese Dave and Big Mike are twenty-eight thousand short."

Then there were the Chinese. Dave then came around and offered my customers a lower price, stealing my clients with my own dope. On top of that, he was shorting me on the cash, knowing that it wasn't always counted right away. We needed several million dollars for the following transaction. It was the first time we'd purchased a hundred keys at once. They planned to knock $2,000 off the price of each key. For a while, we'd been paying 37 for each one. My idea was to save the two thousand dollars several times and then pass the savings on to the homies. It may not seem like much to spend $2000 on each one, but when you're buying hundreds of keys per week, it adds up. Every day, we moved nearly a million dollars in drugs, sometimes up to three million dollars. The scope of the operation was incredible. One day in Inglewood, I picked up the newspaper and read, "Earvin (Magic) Johnson has signed a 25-year contract for $1 million per year." He barely makes a million dollars a year, I reasoned. That much was sitting on the bed in the other room. I felt as though I were on top of the world.

It was very understandable. But I didn't need his company, or Big Mike's, or Chinese Dave's; I could sell all the marijuana I had in a few hours. So Ollie and I devised a strategy: once we had the 100 kg, we'd cut Chinese Dave and Big Mike out for a few days to make 'em sweat. That was only the beginning of what was to come for Big Mike and Chinese Dave. I welcomed them back into the fold. They were all seasoned vets. Big Mike was well-versed in everyone and everything that was going on. It was common to pull up to one of his booze businesses and find him chatting to three or four cop cars. I acknowledge that I got some of my low-key persona from Big Mike. If you took him at face value, you'd think he didn't own anything. I assumed he was extremely wealthy, and if he wasn't, he should have been. You couldn't tell just by looking at him. I never saw him wearing new high-end tennis shoes or clothes. It took a long time for me to notice any evidence of wealth.

That only happened the first time I went to Mike's house, and Mike's wealth became clear to me. He lived in Ladera Heights, a posh black neighborhood. The posh area's series of hills was thought to be one of the richest black communities in the world. He had two Benzes in the driveway, one for himself and one for her. My tunes were making so much money by this point, far into 1986, that it was incredible. The majority were making around $100,000 every day. And those were only the guys who sold rocks to vehicles. We were easily shifting between 100 and 200 keys per day. Best of all, save from a few homies I interacted with personally, I was completely off the streets.

The cops had devised a fresh strategy. They walked up to the home instead of driving up to it, which astonished everyone. About 20 men who were peddling on the street fled. It was a complete commotion, with males running in all directions. Norman, who was unskilled at the time, threw the pills into the bushes as he ran. The cops apprehended him and discovered the dope pack. My homegirls reported it was a huge Ziploc bag packed of little crack cocaine chunks—ready rock. I didn't find out how much dope was in the bag until I bailed Norman out of jail; it was a half-kilo! His was a difficult case because he had to be apprehended as well as the bag. However, Norm was acquitted of the accusations due to the defense attorney's superb work.

# CHAPTER 19
# HOMIES AND PRISON

Jocelyn was one of my first customers, and she'd become addicted. I assisted her in getting off the material. As she tried to express, she needed work, so I hired her to do just that: clean houses. She was highly compensated, yet she was always demanding better work. I'd received a phone call from Indian Tommy and Frank. Tommy was doing well in Cincinnati despite only obtaining one or two keys at a time. He bought one and I paid for the other. He didn't have enough money this time to get even the first key. At the same time, I realized it would be difficult to convince one of the homies to travel all the way to Cincinnati to deliver just one key. The homies were insane, squandering money at clubs and craps tables every night. I witnessed them spend $5,000 in one night. That happened several evenings a week. They didn't give a damn about making $2,000 to haul. That was insignificant to them. I told Ollie I needed to buy Tommy some cocaine. "He's waiting for me to return his call." He's curious as to what time we'll arrive. We need to send someone to Cincinnati as soon as possible." Jocelyn was cleaning the home and listening in on my talk with Ollie. She waited as Ollie and I came up with nothing. She ultimately offered to be a courier to Cincinnati, and I gladly accepted. Tommy was familiar to her. They'd even gotten high together.

It was going to be an eventful night. I always get a stomach ache when I send dope on long travels. For stressful moments like that, I kept a bottle of Mylanta in my back pocket. We returned home after dropping her off at the airport. Evenings were usually a guessing game as to who I'd be spending the night with. A lot of it had to do with who I'd seen the most recently and who I'd seen the least recently. Marilyn was my girl that night. Ollie drove me to her house. When I awoke the next morning, I hurried straight to Mary's for Jocelyn's word. Nobody had heard anything from her. It had been about eight hours; she should have been there and on her way back home by now. I dialed Tommy's number. Tommy described what had happened to Jocelyn. She had missed a cab at the Cincinnati airport in Florence, Kentucky, just across the state line. The DEA intercepted her as she was about to get into the cab and arrested her. All I could think was that someone in Tommy's team had informed the federal narcs. It wasn't like drug-sniffing dogs had discovered the stash. It wasn't a big airport. Agents had also searched her without a warrant. Alan Fenster was hired to represent her. It took 30 days and a $30,000 bond to get her out of jail. For approximately two years, she traveled back and forth from Los Angeles to Cincinnati for court hearings. Due to the improper search and seizure, the charges were eventually withdrawn. Jocelyn continued to work for me as a housekeeper and cleaner.

In late 1986, the cops finally caught up with me, and it was the same Los Angeles County Sheriff's deputies who had been after me for years. It happened one night when Ollie, Cornell, and I were leaving the Big Palace of Wheels. We made our way to my Ford LTD station wagon, which I'd parked in a back alley because I knew the cops were usually hunting for me. As I went along 74th Street, I spotted a car rushing up behind me with its lights turned off. I knew the cop car was traveling quickly because I was doing the same. "I'm gonna lose 'em," I said to Ollie and Cornell. But I got stuck at a red light.

At least one deputy fired bullets at me as I rushed toward a yard. I could hear gunshots zipping over my head. No one yelled, "Freeze," "Police," or "Put up your hands." Nothing except gunfire. I hopped over a fence, came to a halt, and then reversed my path, moving to the front of the yard while they walked around the back, where they thought I'd be running. I misplaced them. I walked to Western, where a city bus was about to arrive. I got off the bus in Gaines, walked to a pay phone, and called Marilyn. She drove me to my condo on

Sepulveda and Ventura Boulevard—a superb location in a wealthy neighborhood where mansions were selling for a million dollars. I took cover there. I'd be sitting in County with Ollie and Cornell if it hadn't been for my street smarts and a lot of luck. Worse, I'd be dead as a result of gunshot wounds. It didn't feel right having Ol' in jail; he and I had been friends since we were kids, and he was the one who got me into the drug game.

When my beeper went off, I was relaxing in my bedroom, waiting to hear from both Jocelyn and Marilyn. Jocelyn was there. I leapt to my feet, dashed outside to a nearby phone booth, and dialed her number. She virtually shrieked when she told me the news: both bails had been posted. Despite the fact that the bond cost me $70,000, I was happy they were being released. I was lying down in my bedroom, trying to make sense of what had happened the night before, when I heard a knock at the door. Who could it possibly be? Only a few people were aware of this location. I'd dispatched Marilyn to handle the paperwork for Ollie and Cornell, leaving me alone. I wasn't expecting her to return so quickly. I crept up to the door, my breath held, and peered out. June and Steve were two young cats, maybe 18 and 19. They were undoubtedly looking for me. They'd been doing it since they were 15 years old, staying where I stayed. These two kids were fierce and would defend me with their lives; it was like having six eyes. I noticed a police cruiser stopped at a red signal as we walked down the street. I'd put on my disguise. I'd shaved my beard and was wearing sunglasses. We walked immediately in front of their automobile, almost touching. We knew they were watching, so we strolled through Denny's to the Ventura Mall just in case. They continued on, and we turned around and returned to Denny's.

Back at the condo, it was around 2 p.m. when I met up with Ollie and Cornell, who told me what happened after I ran. He explained that when I leaped out of the driver's side of the car while it was driving, he had to slide over and stop it from crashing into a home. What would have occurred if I had been found with their drugs, I wondered? Then Kenny sent me a message. When I called, he stated my mother needed to speak with me. When I called home, she stated that cops had been at her house all night and that they'd been broadcasting on the TV that I had shot at cops, that I was sought, and that I was armed and dangerous. The bad news was that they'd filed charges against me not only for that night, but also for other alleged offenses I'd committed in the past. My bail was set at one million dollars. I could easily make bail. But in order to post that, I needed $1.2 million in property and $100,000 in cash. While I had property and cash, an amendment to a legislation known as the 1251 had been passed, which specified that if you put up property, it could not have been earned by drug earnings. Bail had to be approved by a judge, who would have the property and cash investigated. So I needed $1.2 million in equity and a $100,000 cheque from someone who could prove it was properly obtained. This was not a simple task. The majority of my friends didn't own their own homes. I was pleasantly delighted when my mom's neighbors stepped up and said they'd put their properties up for sale for me. We only had $700,000 and change after all was said and done.

Alan summoned me to his office for a meeting. He made me go via the back so I wouldn't be spotted in case it was being watched. While I was there, he called the D.A.'s office and requested that bail be reduced to $100,000, but they refused. So we moved to Plan B, which was to appear before the black judge whose courtroom the case had been assigned and request a $500,000 bail reduction. Alan made a statement right before our meeting ended that led me to assume he didn't believe the officers planted the drugs and lied about me shooting a revolver at them. "Rick, I want you to go take a lie detector test," he stated.

I was nervous even before they attached the wires to me. The tester was a middle-aged white man who was balding on top. He informed me that the test was only 95% accurate. All I wanted him to say was that I was innocent and that the cops were telling the truth. When Alan called the next day to tell me the findings, I was surprised when he asked, "Did you have cocaine on you the night of the chase, because that question came back positive?" I promised to him that I hadn't. The good news was that when I was asked if I had shot at the cops, the test revealed that I had not lied when I said "No." However, this did not prevent the lawsuit from proceeding. I chose to turn myself in after consulting with my attorney, Alan Fenster. Alan had warned me about cops trying to arrest me in front of the courthouse before I was supposed to surrender. My attorney contacted the district attorney's office and arranged for me to surrender in order to avoid a public spectacle in which detectives perform "perp walks," in which they parade defendants in front of the media as they walk them into court or to booking. I hadn't expected that, so I disguised myself by trimming my beard and donning a baseball cap.

As Alan, my mother, my homie Lil Stevie, and I sat in the seats lined the hallway outside the courtroom, two narcotics police man stood 10 feet away, staring at me. I could see them out of the corner of my eye and hoped that my disguise was effective. Lil Stevie walked closer to them so he could hear what they were saying. The cops relaxed when I stood up to go to the men's restroom. Lil Steve followed me to tell me what he'd overheard. But as soon as I went out of the restroom, the bailiff opened the courtroom doors. It was packed from a previous session. On Monday mornings, municipal court was always like that, and there were only three rows of seats in the courtroom. The cops were stationed on the prosecution's side of the courtroom, as if a boundary had been drawn.

Alan advocated for a reduction of my bail, but the judge denied it. I was then admitted to the county jail in downtown Los Angeles, block 4800, in the gang module, despite the fact that I was not a gangbanger. The D.A. charged me with a slew of fake felonies, including firing at an officer and fleeing the scene of a crime. Alan Fenster then requested a copy of the tape from the court, which the judge allowed. The recording was provided to Alan almost immediately. Alan contacted a professional to examine the tape. In turn, the court dismissed all accusations against me for police misconduct based on the officers insulting my counsel to me and the tape given to the court having a significant chunk cut out. Because of the changed tape produced in court and the fact that they'd planted drugs in my car, I not only beat the charge, but the information Alan and I acquired helped spark a federal corruption probe into the sheriff's officers' behavior. It took Frenchy, the private investigator we hired, nearly a year to receive confirmation of the planted evidence. Frenchy handed over his reports to Alan, who turned everything over to the FBI, including the tampered-with tape.

Despite the fact that I had been liberated and set free, I desired a change. I made the decision to go to Cincinnati, Ohio, with Marilyn and our little daughter. Marilyn needs to stop using drugs. And I needed to unwind. We settled in a quiet community on Cincinnati's east side. Danilo Blandón approached me again after I'd been out of the cocaine industry for approximately a year while living in Cincinnati. He proposed a cut from the 130 kg he needed to distribute. I was familiar with the area because I had lived in Cincinnati for some time. I re-entered the fray and eventually dominated Cincinnati's crack market with Danilo as my supply. I traveled back and forth to Los Angeles, reopening and supervising my operations in both cities.

The homies, including JJ, a cousin from Texas, were now in command. I recall JJ's first day in California. He'd been living in a trailer house in rural Texas, where there were no lights and you had to be careful not to fall through the floor. He was living in what we dubbed "dirt-ball" conditions, so I gave him a chance. I started him off like everyone else, giving him an ounce of dope and some training before directing him to the track. JJ displayed characteristics that none of the other homies displayed. He assisted Ollie and me when he ran out of his product. He even stopped drinking for a short time. He was moving quickly. We'd use the same dope game approach to manage the motels I owned. The first three drug deals were supposed to cover the cost of more lodgings. We were also working on a handful of apartment rehabs, as well as a 32-unit apartment complex. I'd been spending money, but it had all been for investments. We'd be back on track once I finished the projects.

As usual, I had business to attend to and didn't have time to continue looking for him. I gathered Paul, Zo, and Tootie for a 100-kilo purchase. We always bought dope with an entourage. We had a better chance of escaping if something went wrong. And we always had the site scoped out and planned out so that no one could rob us. Paul was the primary motivator back then. He'd drive with a loaded ride right next to a cop car and not blink an eye. I called Ollie, who was now out on bail, to make sure he had the money. By then, that was pretty much all he and my brother David did. When the money homes reached a couple hundred thousand, they would pick it up and take it to the stash house. We'd been taking orders from the main players all day. We have no unsatisfied customers. Zo seemed to know everyone that JJ did.

A few minutes later, while shooting hoops at Manchester Park, I overheard some kids reporting that JJ had converted the Hoover Crip and was running around 81st and Hoover passing out wads of cash. I called the boys and informed them of what I had heard. Everyone agreed that JJ had been behaving strangely during the last few days. And Lil' Steve informed me that $80,000 had gone missing from JJ's stash container. This was a difficult one for me. JJ was my guy. But I couldn't let anyone, relative or not, take my money and throw it away. Then things got worse. When I came into the shop's driveway, Kenny and Tootie ran up and told me that JJ, Eric, and Jeta had just whooped on our kids Steve and NY, trying to find the money car so he could steal more. I was sweltering. These were mature men attacking teenagers. My tiny homies refused to sing, and they suffered a pounding as a result. It never occurred to me that my main guys were planning a coup while the rest were picking sides. I couldn't believe it when it finally hit me. I mean, I'd brought all of these people in when the majority of them didn't have a penny and were pleading with me for assistance. I'd always worked well with others. That was part of my plan: to get everything set up for the entire team so that we'd be ready for the rest of our lives. I understood what they were going through: money, petty jealousies, jockeying for status, dirty cops, clean cops, and legal issues. I realized how difficult it was for them to see millions pass through their hands while earning only worker's salaries. It was all coming to a climax, and now I'd have to deal with internal swindles, backstabbing, and power struggles. Even though there was a lot going on that night, we cooked as usual. We'd only been at 62nd Street for a few weeks. It was an all-brick structure, and I'd spent $40,000 barring it up to keep it safe. We cooked the most recent batch all night. I scheduled a meeting with the guys for the following day in the morning. I was irritated and wanted to get it out of the way.

Carolyn, whose aunt was in the car with her, had pulled into the alley and was watching from a distance as I turned around. I felt humiliated. I was very proud of my company and had about a million dollars invested in it. Not only were Carolyn and her aunt watching, but everyone in the car shop could see and hear what was going on. I returned to Carolyn's car, and she informed me that she was leaving. That completely altered my connection with JJ. JJ was gone when I returned to the shop, but not before he'd busted out every windshield in the building. Ollie was still talking about murdering JJ, but I told him it wasn't an option. He remained my cousin. We had a meeting with the crew at Manchester Park's baseball diamond. Except for JJ, everyone, around 30 of us, turned up. I was unsurprised.

I sat back and took everything in. At that point, I decided what I was going to do: cash out the disgruntled guys and slow down. I knew we could do the job without the rest of them. When I totaled everything up, we still had about two million to pay off approximately a dozen guys and let them go. It would just take a few days to recover all of that money. I was ready for the drama to finish so we could get back to business. I was on the verge of leaving the dope game, Lord. When it was my chance to speak again, I proposed what I believed was a reasonable price for everyone to part ways. We agreed on $50,000 each after a brief debate and agreed to meet that night so I could transfer the money. I was broke that night after I paid all the homies their money. We barely scraped together $700,000 when it was time to re-up. We still had money on the street, but it was usually no problem to raise a million and a half or two million and still have money on the street. The pressure was increasing.

I was working on five significant real estate projects at the same time. The cops were arresting my employees left and right; they weren't only targeting my personal crew, but also my customers. Lawyer fees and bail were eating away at me. And the press was starting to pick up on it. Ollie and I stopped by the Inglewood house on the way. When we pulled into the driveway, we noticed a letter on Ollie's boat. The note was from the city and stated that it was too large for the driveway. I'd given Ollie a 40-foot cigarette boat with dual 454 engines for his birthday. It cost me $150,000 to purchase. It was just one more thing to deal with. Then we went to a Mexican restaurant to meet Danilo. From the outside, it didn't appear to be much, but we reasoned that if Danilo chose it, it must be connected, and we'd be safe. It was almost deserted as we walked in.

Danilo informed the owner that we were his friends and that our order would be added to his bill. Two of his companions sat at a different table. Danilo and Henry joined us at our table. I told him that my money was low because I needed to pay the homies. I needed to make some decisions. Part of the issue was that all of the money was going into real estate on two apartment buildings, as well as digging a foundation for the third motel, with a fourth on the way. I'd paid $500,000 for the building, which required approximately $150,000 in repairs and improvements. The plans themselves cost $5,000. But the property would eventually be worth about $2 million, so it was worthwhile. When I applied for permits, I engaged a Beverly Hills lawyer to defend me at the Planning Commission hearing. The previous owner's permits had been canceled for allowing the property to deteriorate and become drug-infested.

Later that night, we met up with Waterhead Bo, a young kid rockin' the streets of Los Angeles, for a round of Ping Pong. I was eager to find out more about his drug game. I was curious as to how many keys he was receiving, how much he was spending, and how he was selling it so cheaply given his inexperience with the game. Back then, only a few drug dealers could afford to spend the amount of money he was. I sat back with Bo and wagered $2,500 on Ping Pong. We talked during the game, and I decided to stop by his place the next day to see about working out a deal. I'd devised another method that required paying Bo a little more, but it was also designed to make my Nicaraguan contact sweat, wondering who my new contact was. It was still daylight when we arrived at Bo's house. Two Latino men stepped out of their car, walked to the trunk, and carried two boxes to us. We all entered the house once Bo opened the door. I was terrified because it was done in broad daylight during the day. Bo had a barred screen on his front door, but it wasn't anything like the heavy-duty material I used.

Then Bo and I reconnected. I admired him, and he admired me. He asked if I wanted to use his internet connection. It took me by surprise. My money was growing quickly, and I had set a goal of getting out of the game and not taking on new business. We'd relocated our operations to West Los Angeles, Brentwood, Westwood, UCLA, and Sherman Oaks in an attempt to escape the heat. I told Bo I'd consider it. The apartments cost us $2,200 each month. One of them served as a meeting point for Danilo and his new sidekick Jose. Danilo and Jose would occasionally spend the night, snort cocaine, and get drunk. I had no idea if they ever had women up there, and it didn't matter to me. I didn't interact with Danilo. It was always all about the money. We rolled out of the parking lot after purchasing a hundred keys from Danilo. Ollie and I exchanged high-fives. Because of all the arrests, our crew had shrunk and our customers had shrunk, but we knew it would catch up—especially with high-quality Colombian products provided through my Nicaraguan connections. We struck a snag after roughly two months of steady rolling when Danilo couldn't provide us. We had a lot of money left over from the previous purchase, so we relaxed for a few days and hit the basketball courts at Manchester Park, just like old times.

During one of my trips to L.A., I purchased another load of cocaine through Bo's link because it was cheaper there, to tide us over until I could get more from Danilo. I placed a homie—a friend of a friend—on a bus in Los Angeles, then flew back to Cincinnati to meet him. We didn't find out until later that the cocaine was discovered by a drug-sniffing dog at a New Mexico bus terminal during one of the stops along the journey. The cocaine was then traced to me by DEA investigators based on witness accounts rather than physical evidence. Based on such comments, I was charged with narcotics trafficking in 1989. I accepted a plea agreement for cocaine trafficking and received a mandatory 10-year prison sentence, which I served in a facility in Boone County, Kentucky, across the Ohio

River from Cincinnati, where federal and state convicts were kept together. Then, in November 1993, while still in detention in Cincinnati, a warrant for my arrest was issued from Smith County, Texas, based on an interception of a phone call four years earlier, in 1988, in which police said I agreed to give two keys of cocaine to my cousin in Tyler, Texas. As a result, they linked the case to me. I pleaded no guilty to conspiracy to possess cocaine and was sentenced to a brief term that ran concurrently with my federal time in Ohio.

They needed additional witnesses against the former task force detectives, so they offered me a deal: help them convict the elite narcotics squad—including the cops who shot at me and planted drugs in my car. In exchange, they would get my prison time in Ohio lowered. They wanted me to explain about the task force's searches of crack homes, how much money they'd seized, and who they'd battered during their operations. The government flew me to Los Angeles to testify. It was a successful day in L.A. Superior Court. I'd taken the stand to testify against the officers who had hounded me and harassed my employees for years. The Los Angeles Times referred to me as a "key witness." When I testified against once-respected and experienced narcotics investigators, I revealed the truth. I was relieved. I was guilty of selling drugs, but not of having the cocaine that the cops planted in my car that night. In exchange for my testimony, the court lowered my 10-year sentence to 51 months, with three years of supervised release after that. In addition, the authorities agreed not to seize my residual narcotics profits.

After I was paroled from Texas in September 1994, I returned to South Central. I still had the Big Palace of Wheels plus some money in the bank. Cincinnati was the last place I sold drugs.I didn't return to selling cocaine. I continued to run the Big Palace of Wheels, plus I had cash on hand. I was turning my life around. I didn't know where Danilo Blandón was, and I didn't care. I was out of the game.

# CHAPTER 20
# REVERSE STING OPERATION

After being released from prison for a few months, I kept myself busy with my properties and a theater refurbishment. I made a lot of money from the motels and used it to buy more properties. In addition, I was in the process of purchasing the historic Adams Street Theatre and converting it into a youth center. I'd been approaching community leaders for financial assistance. And I was just starting out in the record business, attempting to sign artists. I was starting my own rap label at the time, and I'd discovered the Alkoholiks. We were in talks, and I was going to sign them. Dick Griffey and Otis Smith, two strong heavyweights in the music industry at the time, had pushed me into sponsoring R&B vocalist Anita Baker years before.

Then a call came in that I didn't want or expect: Danilo Blandón contacted me about supplying me with cocaine again. He'd been my major supplier for years, but I subsequently learned he'd been arrested and charged with conspiracy to possess cocaine with the purpose to distribute, so I'd lost him as a source for at least two years. When I returned to Los Angeles following my prison sentence, Danilo chased me to buy from him again. He worked me out for six months. At the time, I was still convinced that Danilo was motivated by money. I was sorely mistaken.

It felt fantastic negotiating a solid business agreement as I walked out of Griffey's office on Wilshire after discussing signing artists. Then I answered Danilo's call. He wanted me to meet him at a restaurant in downtown Los Angeles. I planned to meet him just like I would any of my other guys. I was out of the game and had no intention of returning. Even though the immediate cash was appealing, I refused to even schedule the purchase. I'd seen what I was capable of doing legally on the streets. I was freed of the stress of running an illicit business. Danilo had always given me good prices, and now he was in difficulties; it was the least I could do. So, as a favor to Danilo, I broke down and agreed to introduce him to a friend. It was a one-time occurrence, and I would still be out of the game. I found a buyer in my friend Chico Brown, who had constructed his own game while I was in prison. I knew he'd want Danilo's coke. I also hoped that if I gave him Chico's contact information, Danilo would back off and not force me to buy from him again.

So, on March 2, 1995, the transaction took place in a shopping center parking lot in Chula Vista, a San Diego suburb. Mike and I exited his truck, opened the back of the switch car, and took the drug bag. Curtis later informed me that was when he noticed men's heads popping up inside parked cars. The DEA and municipal authorities swarmed all over us the moment the deal was completed. I ran and ran until my breath ran out. In a backyard, an army of men dressed in suits and uniforms surrounded me. Even when a cop put his foot on the back of my neck, I didn't feel any discomfort. I was out of breath after running so hard. It felt like I was back in the chop shop, fleeing the cops a lifetime ago.

It wasn't until a reporter from the San Jose Mercury News, Gary Webb, interviewed me in prison and broke the bombshell that I realized how important Danilo was. Gary questioned me after his visit and several phone calls, "What would you say if I told you he was working for the CIA and Contras, selling cocaine to help them buy weapons and supplies?" I was taken aback. First and foremost, I'd never heard of the Contras, an alliance of rebels that helped destroy the Somoza government in Nicaragua, then felt betrayed and afterwards attacked the ruling Sandinistas. But, more importantly, Danilo had been selling all of this coke while I was in jail. I was taken aback. Even still, it took me a while to accept that Danilo

Blandón, whom I considered a friend and nearly a godfather, had been working for the CIA to bring me down. Gary gave documentation to my attorney to aid in my court case. Gary knew significantly more about the CIA's role, as well as Danilo and his drug partner, Norwin Meneses, who worked out of San Francisco, while Blandón worked out of Los Angeles. I'd heard the name Meneses mentioned in passing by Danilo throughout the years.

Gary sat in the front row of the courtroom, behind the defense table, throughout the duration of my trial, which began in 1996. Alan Fenster, my defense attorney, placed a high value on Gary. Alan occasionally asked him for advice on what questions to ask the witnesses. Despite Gary's assistance, an all-white jury found me guilty and sentenced me to prison for conspiracy to distribute illegal substances. We recognized then that I had most likely been enticed to San Diego County for the reverse sting operation since a narcotics arrest in Los Angeles would have meant a downtown Los Angeles jury, with a few black jurors more likely than not.

On November 19, 1996, approximately 20 months after the government sting operation that landed me in jail, I was seated at the defense table next to Alan Fenster in U.S. District Court in the tightly guarded, crowded courtroom. As Judge Huff ordered me to do my term in the Lompoc Federal Penitentiary, I stood up, my wrists and feet shackled and dressed in a khaki prison jumpsuit. Despite the fact that I was not a violent offender, she sent me to a maximum-security institution in central California that was previously a World War II disciplinary camp. The ninth floor, where I was held, was largely occupied by Mexican Mafia gang members. Those guys didn't usually get along with their brothers, but they just showed me love.

I wasn't the only inmate running an illegal commissary in the prison compound; throughout my time at MCC, approximately 50 or 60 offenders ran unofficial stores for inmates. The difference was that the Mexican Mafia bosses let their homies buy from me. I was on the ninth floor of MCC for six years before being relocated to the Lompoc federal facility, dubbed The New Rock because an Alcatraz boulder now rests outside the prison. At Lompoc, I wore a red wristband, which meant I had to be observed 24 hours a day and had to check in with a guard every hour while on labor duty. I was assigned to a janitorial team along the corridor, directly across from the lieutenant and captain's offices. Thirty of us with red wristbands were allocated to that hallway, where we cleaned a 50-foot-long by four-foot-wide strip.

The only time I got in trouble in the pen was for "doing business." It happened when I was on the phone, which was being monitored by security. Even though I had only talked about cutting albums and creating videos with rappers, any outside business conversations were forbidden. As punishment, I was placed in solitary confinement, sometimes known as the hole, several times for periods ranging from two weeks to 45 days. I read and did a lot of push-ups in the hole. I also recovered from years of sleep deprivation. Solitary inmates learn to sleep a lot. Back in my MCC cell after court, I vowed to right the mistake and clear my name. I was imprisoned and ignorant. To contest the sentence, I needed to be able to read in order to research my own case in the prison law library.

The Malcolm X Autobiography and Anthony Robbins' Awaken the Giant Within were the first books I read cover to cover. Then I read Napoleon Hill's Think and Grow Rich and George Clayson's The Richest Man in Babylon, two of the best self-help books ever produced in my opinion. My entire worldview shifted. I began to see the world in a new light. Reading those books literally saved my life. Then there was my appeal on the grounds of double jeopardy, or being sentenced twice for the same offense. Inmates assisted me in my case. Because of my background, I was respected in prison.

I was resentenced and condemned to 20 years in prison, with almost half of that time remaining. Despite the fact that it was still a long time, knowing I wasn't in for life gave me something to look forward to. I was released in March 2009 and sent immediately to a halfway house in San Diego's Lincoln Heights neighborhood, where I resided with around 200 other federal and state criminals. I was relocated to El Monte, California, halfway home two months before my post-prison time was done. I was released from custody in September 2009 and returned to Los Angeles under the supervision of the parole office. My parole was for seven years and will expire in late 2016.

In a New York Times story, Katz stated, "If there was an eye to the storm, if there was a criminal mastermind behind crack's decade-long reign, if there was one outlaw capitalist most responsible for flooding Los Angeles' streets with mass-marketed cocaine, his name was Freeway Rick." Katz came to San Diego to interview me at the federal penitentiary in downtown San Diego. In a later article for Texas Monthly, Katz said that Danilo "Blandón's tenuous ties to the Contras were already severed by the time he met Rick," and that "Rick already was a big player by the time he met Blandón." Furthermore, according to Jesse Katz, "no evidence could be found to link either Rick or Blandón to the CIA......"

The three-day series in the Times did not harm my reputation, but it did permanently harm Gary Webb's. The newspaper slammed his reporting on the Contra scandal. The Mercury News initially supported Gary. But, in the midst of the media frenzy, the paper recanted. Gary's journalism career was ruined. I was enraged after reading the stories Jesse Katz wrote about Gary and called Jesse from prison to tell him what I thought of them. In the end, Gary Webb was vindicated by a 1998 CIA Inspector General report, which revealed that the CIA had covered up a financial relationship it had with Nicaraguan drug dealers, especially Danilo Blandón and others, for more than a decade. It was too little, too late for Gary. His marriage was over, and his career as a national reporter was over.

Danilo Blandón, on the other hand, was facing up to four life sentences at one point. Instead, he struck a bargain: help arrest Freeway Rick in exchange for doing less time. Danilo was granted a green card and the right to remain in the country after testifying for the prosecution during my San Diego trial. He'd been in the country illegally and was a convicted felon for drug trafficking, which meant he'd be deported without a hearing—at least for everyone else. Blandón was issued a coveted green card by the government. According to my knowledge, only the Attorney General or the President of the United States may make it happen. Danilo, who now has permanent residency, was released from prison after 28 months. Meanwhile, I began serving a life sentence that was eventually reversed on a technicality.

At the time, I saw no other options for an illiterate high school and junior college dropout with a broken-down car and a mother who worked two jobs simply to put food on the table in South Central. I felt bound by my circumstances, which included losing a potential sports scholarship the moment the coach discovered I couldn't read and write. So I did what I believed I needed to do to survive. I wound up as a teen in an illicit enterprise, running about South Central with duffel bags full of cash. Though it was not the finest career path, I treated drug trafficking as a full-time job, just as I would have if it had been a real business.

Needless to say, I'm no longer in the drug trade. I'm an entrepreneur that represents musicians and athletes in the music and sports industries, as well as a speaker who visits schools across the country. I go to ghetto schools and tell students and young people that there are alternatives to a life of crime. I tell them to stay straight and work hard in order to be successful in life. I convey that sense of helplessness to kids in the neighborhood. Today, I teach economics to students in a continuation high school in Los Angeles' Watts neighborhood, as well as lecture at other schools across the country. I am a drug lord who has paid my obligation to society. I intend to keep giving back to my community. In addition, I volunteer to feed the homeless in downtown Los Angeles. I tell the tale of my life as Freeway to high school and college students all throughout the country. Rick Ross, your writings and information helped me reform, change my life for the better, and contest the severe sentence I received for a nonviolent offense. Regardless of the challenges people experience, books can alter their lives; knowledge is power. I can't change the bad influence crack cocaine had on my neighborhood, its people, or the role I played in it. I didn't start distributing narcotics because I wanted to wreak havoc on my town; I sold cocaine because I needed to get out of poverty. Today, I set a good example. I have not sold narcotics in over 20 years. I encourage inner-city youngsters that they must make informed decisions, stay in school, keep clean, and be cheerful. They can't do it by gangbanging or dealing. That is my message, and that is my legacy.

Made in United States
Troutdale, OR
07/25/2024

21524605R00080